Helping Your Child with PDA Live a Happier Life

of related interest

**Pathological Demand Avoidance Syndrome
– My Daughter is Not Naughty**
Jane Alison Sherwin
ISBN 978 1 84905 614 4
eISBN 978 1 78450 085 6

**Being Julia - A Personal Account of Living
with Pathological Demand Avoidance**
Ruth Fidler and Julia Daunt
Foreword by Dr Judy Eaton
ISBN 978 1 84905 681 6
eISBN 978 1 78450 188 4

**The PDA Paradox
The Highs and Lows of My Life on a Little-
Known Part of the Autism Spectrum**
Harry Thompson
Foreword by Felicity Evans
ISBN 978 1 78592 675 4
eISBN 978 1 78592 677 8

Me and My PDA
A Guide to Pathological Demand Avoidance for Young People
Glòria Durà-Vilà and Tamar Levi
ISBN 978 1 78592 465 1
eISBN 978 1 78450 849 4

Helping Your Child with PDA Live a Happier Life

Alice Running

Jessica Kingsley Publishers
London and Philadelphia

First published in Great Britain in 2022 by Jessica Kingsley Publishers
An Hachette Company

1

Copyright © Alice Running 2021

Front cover image source: Shutterstock®. The cover image is for
illustrative purposes only, and any person featuring is a model.

A CIP catalogue record for this title is available from the
British Library and the Library of Congress

ISBN 978 1 78775 485 0
eISBN 978 1 78775 486 7

Printed and bound in Great Britain by Clays Ltd

Jessica Kingsley Publishers' policy is to use papers that are natural,
renewable and recyclable products and made from wood grown in sus-
tainable forests. The logging and manufacturing processes are expected
to conform to the environmental regulations of the country of origin.

Jessica Kingsley Publishers
Carmelite House
50 Victoria Embankment
London EC4Y 0DZ

www.jkp.com

Dedicated to my two wonderful sons, who are both perfect and whom I love so very much.

And to Charlie, the best dog.

Acknowledgements

I would like to thank my family for their unwavering support. They have provided strength and solidarity during all the many difficult meetings I have had while trying to advocate for my children. I would like to thank my mother, who has provided endless (free) caring support to my children when local services have not.

I would also like to thank Helen, and all the other support groups who offer genuine understanding, good advice and expertise – if only those in power would listen to the autism community more.

Contents

Introduction

Setting Pathological Demand Avoidance in Context

Pathological demand avoidance (PDA) is increasingly becoming recognized as a distinct, neurological difference that is part of the autism spectrum – pathological demand avoidance is an autism spectrum condition. However, PDA is not yet identified via current diagnostic criteria for autism and so many people receive a diagnosis of autism with demand avoidance, instead of a diagnosis of pathological demand avoidance in its own right.

Many children receive a diagnosis of autism but then go on to find that this diagnosis does not necessarily address all challenges experienced during daily life. Pathological demand avoidance can be explained as a permanent struggle with one's internal self, leading to automatic resistance to demands made of us. Demands can be as seemingly trivial as using the toilet or speaking. Resistance to demands is not a choice and is related to how a neurodiverse mind is expected to cope within an intolerable, neurotypical world.

A PDA mind is an autistic mind and will share similar experiences in relation to interacting with non-autistic people and environments – intolerable sensory experiences, communication differences, detailed focus and alternative social imagination. But a PDA mind may find typical 'autism-friendly' approaches and strategies painful to experience, resulting in an increased distress response. In my opinion, this is why it is so important to distinctly categorize 'PDA' as a presentation. Using traditional autism interventions and strategies may be as harmful to a PDA child as using traditional neurotypical parenting approaches. For a PDA child, life is experienced in permanent anxiety and this fear is exacerbated through having things done *to* them, rather than *with* them. Collaboration is key to engagement – and to collaborate successfully with a PDA child, we must first understand the world from their point of view.

Pathological demand avoidance is a neurological difference and children who are diagnosed with PDA are 'born this way'. There is significant debate within the autism community with regards to pathological demand avoidance as a separate, diagnostic identity. Some autistic people feel that demand avoidance is a rational response, rooted in anxiety at having to operate within a non-autism-friendly world or environment. There are many autistic people who consider demand avoidance to be a trauma response to misguided autism interventions. This book does not focus on these debates but aims to offer practical advice, based on real-life experience, with the aim of making life happier for autistic children with demand avoidance as part of their interaction with the world.

I am autistic. I have two autistic children who experience levels of anxiety to such a degree that life can become intolerable for them. They have both been professionally assessed as fitting the criteria for pathological demand avoidance. Unfortunately, in the area in which we live, our local authority does not recognize PDA as a distinct part of the autism spectrum and tends to explain complexities as behavioural or exacerbated by poor parenting. It is a difficult position to be in, as advocating in your child's best interests can place you in direct opposition with those who have a duty of care for your child (health, education, social care). I have experienced first-hand how the wrong type of environment or wrong teaching approach can disable my children in a way that their autistic minds will never do. An autistic or PDA mind is not an innate disabler, but how outside, societal interventions treat an autistic person can be extremely disabling.

Behavioural or corrective interventions can be extremely damaging to an autistic mind, as perceived 'behaviour' is essentially a communication of distress that something is intolerable to our neurodiversity. Cognitive behavioural therapies and applied behavioural analysis aim to retrain thought processes, and subsequent behavioural responses. But if the 'cause' of the 'behaviour' that needs addressing is essentially how an autistic mind experiences an environment that is not inclusive, then no behavioural change will ever occur without the disabling environment adapting to the needs of an autistic mind.

In mainstream school my children simply could not cope. The noise, the constant anxiety at not being able to effectively connect with the people around them and the permanent demands to do so left them distraught and traumatized at a very young age. The only way forward for our family at this juncture was to remove them from the school environment and allow this heightened distress to naturally dissipate. Their mental health took priority over their academic journey for several years, and without this intervention it is likely that they both would have become extremely ill indeed. When distress gets too high, it can become impossible to manage, and until anxiety has reduced holistically, no approach will be helpful.

In my experience, utilizing the approach of demand reduction (in order for recovery to happen) is not welcomed by some professionals, who often view this approach as neglectful or enabling. However, conversations around PDA are becoming more commonplace within all relevant professional fields and there are several 'champions' (in social care, psychology and education) who advocate well for the specific needs of PDA children. In a sense, many of our children are pioneers, gradually challenging the traditional practice methods of established 'experts'. As a parent, this can be an extremely isolating position to be in – there is no quick fix that will suddenly make our children behave in a way that is considered desirable by these professionals. We know that our parenting is filled with love and a desire for our children to be happy, but we also know that using reward charts and naughty steps will not help. As parents, we are blamed for not being firm enough or for not having boundaries or structure in our homes, yet we know that these approaches can lead to more distress and more resistance from our children. Instead, we offer creativity, patience, good humour and flexibility. On more than one occasion it has been said to me that I am indulgent, enabling their avoidance by my therapeutic parenting approach. It often feels as if I am in a lose-lose situation.

It would be wonderful to be able to avoid such scrutiny and be allowed to focus entirely on the needs of our children, but the characteristics of distress for a PDA child are also considered to be identifiers of abuse by safeguarding professionals. A traditional safeguarding approach appropriates blame on parenting approaches, parental mental health and familial dynamics instead of recognizing the unique needs of a PDA child.

Appropriating blame in this way systematically disempowers our parental ability to act as advocates for our children. For me, this is why it is so important to make space for authentic autistic voices to be heard.

Many of the difficulties faced by autistic people and their families stem from the outside world viewing autism as a medical condition. Categorizing autism within this medical model of disability means that autism is often treated via a medical pathway, with mental health or behavioural interventions often used in an attempt to acquire 'improvement'. Striving for 'improvement' can be misguided – yes, we want our children to be happy and live fulfilling lives by reaching their potential, but 'improvement' is so often measured against a neurotypical benchmark. Expecting autistic minds to respond differently to stimuli that are intolerable due to our innate neurology (by undertaking a course of cognitive behavioural therapy, for example) is unreasonable – and dangerous. What happens when our children do not 'improve' to the standard required by professionals?

Autism assessments for children are still conducted under mental health services, despite autism being entirely neurological. This can lead to misdiagnosis or missed diagnosis, particularly in relation to autistic children who have a demand avoidant presentation or deviate from the stereotypical profile of autism (autistic women and girls can often struggle to obtain a correct diagnosis of autism).

The difficulties my children and I have encountered in obtaining good and accurate diagnoses of autism have been extreme but are sadly not that unusual. Being able to communicate verbally and being identified as academically able at school meant that their early years schooling did not recognize that they were struggling socially and with the school environment.

At school, my children would tolerate their environment but then release their frustrations at home, with me. This quickly led to school categorizing my children as 'having problems at home' – a descriptor that has been almost impossible to get rid of, even with 'official' autism diagnoses. With school being unable to recognize their needs as autistic children, their pathway to assessment was a battle over many years, with referrals first being made to parenting courses, parenting support and mental health services. It took several attempts to even have my children placed on the waiting list for autism assessments.

After years of my children being held on the waiting list for assessments, we found that diagnostic conclusions were still evasive on the first assessments. Diagnostically, autistic 'traits' do not need to be observable in all environments for a conclusion to be made. My children both exceeded the clinical thresholds for autism during their ADOS (Autism Diagnostic Observation Schedule – a standardized set of observations) assessments, but diagnoses were withheld due to lack of pervasiveness. Essentially, 'Mum's record of their developmental history' did not match school observations. Again, this is a worrying trend within current autism diagnostic methods. Many, many children do not receive a diagnosis because they are able to blend in and suppress their needs in the few hours spent at school. This leads to many children not receiving accurate diagnoses and many children receiving late diagnoses, therefore missing out on years of essential early years support. More dangerously, there are accounts of some families having to contend with accusations from child protection services that they are fabricating or exaggerating their children's presentation – and all because of some professionals not fully understanding how autistic children may present differently at school and at home.

In my opinion, the current diagnostic process relies too

heavily on teaching professionals making accurate observations regarding autism. Autism awareness within the teaching profession has grown, but there is no overall, national consistency in practice – you may be lucky enough to have knowledgeable teachers supporting an autism assessment for your child or you may be extremely unlucky and have teachers who blame you as a parent. This is not a just process, and the way in which children are assessed for autism and other neurodiversity needs to be extensively reviewed.

I had not heard of pathological demand avoidance when I first began to request an autism assessment for my eldest son. After being told that he did not require an autism assessment, I took some time to conduct extensive research. I discovered a television series that followed several children undertaking autism assessments, one of whom was diagnosed with PDA. I recall being amazed at how similar this child was to my own child – both were remarkable and unique, but their challenges with regards to daily life and their responses to these challenges were similar enough for me to ask my local NHS autism pathway whether they would assess my son via the PDA profile. It took a while to obtain an answer, but a clinical psychologist did speak with me about seeking a PDA-specific assessment. He said that it was not a fully recognized condition and that many of the identifying characteristics overlapped with an Asperger's Syndrome profile. He also said that trying to source support for a PDA child would be impossible as there was so little awareness and understanding. I accepted this opinion at the time, but life experience has taught me that without diagnostic or clinical recognition of demand avoidance, and how it relates to autism, it is our children who ultimately suffer through the needless application of tortuous interventions and strategies.

As a mother, I was filled with joy and relief when my children received their autism diagnoses – joy at the possibilities of them being able to connect with a community and seek fulfilment through their identities, and selfish relief at having a concrete reason (other than my supposedly bad parenting) for why certain aspects of life were so difficult for them. In my naivety, I felt that their diagnoses would open a plethora of help and understanding which would enable them to lead happy lives. Many families do get the right help that they need: specialist educational placements, access to knowledgeable psychologists and psychiatrists, and adapted environments. For other families, life after diagnosis can become increasingly frustrating as professionals continue to gatekeep precious funding and resources and steer autistic children into generalized, rather than specialist, support pathways.

With the right professionals on my children's team, life has been calm and stress-free. When their presentations have been respected and both their aspirations and anxieties listened to, they have been happy children who have made good connections with the outside world. When professionals have sought unrealistic expectations and cited parenting as a barrier to progress, then my children have suffered – they have become withdrawn and unable to self-regulate their emotions.

There have been times when my views and the views of professionals working with my children have been different. For example, both of my children find the noise of the vacuum cleaner painful. My eldest son responds to its use by screaming and covering his ears. My youngest son responds by laughing hysterically and bounding over furniture. I have requested sensory occupational therapy assessments for both of my children and been informed that (in our area) there is no way of obtaining such an assessment via the NHS. Seeking to help my children cope with such a regular necessity, I bought them ear defenders or vacuumed when they were out of the house (which is very infrequently), only to be told that this was not helping them to be able to manage in the 'real world'. 'What will happen when they hear a vacuum cleaner when they're at work or college? They can't run around screaming then?' And so, I am very often viewed as an indulgent mother for enabling them to exist outside the 'real world' instead of helping them to tolerate it. This professional point of view seems so instinctively wrong to me. Struggling along in distress and pain, just to please others, will have a detrimental impact on their mental health over the long term. Surely, we should be teaching our children how to advocate for themselves and teach them the skills to request reasonable adjustments rather than asking them to 'shut up and put up'. I gave up trying to obtain a sensory assessment and I gave up requesting that they wear ear defenders when I vacuum. I bought a carpet sweeper instead (and a push rotary lawnmower). I want my children to feel safe and welcome in their own home and for that reason I will continue to adapt our home and way of life.

I have been navigating the world of autism service provision for some time now; my eldest son is fast approaching adulthood. 'Support systems' are pockets of severely underfunded and overstretched services that are loosely connected to one another and vary greatly from geographical area to area – there is little national cohesion. Unless you are privileged enough to source independent (private) assessments and services, then it is possible that your child will be provided with the bare minimum. 'Support systems' do not operate in a preventative way – and by this, I mean that your child has to be struggling and in crisis before 'help' is provided. If our schools and societies were inclusive of autistic minds by design, or reasonable adjustments were made in good time (and parents were listened to early enough), then our children would not need to enter into crisis and their mental health would be given adequate protection. As parents, it can sometimes feel as if our children are not receiving the right support from those services and professionals we turn to for help. We know that our children are talented and unique people who have a lot to offer the world, if only the world could be more receptive and flexible. The onus should not be on how to 'treat' or 'fix' our children in order for them to fit in but rather on how to create environments in which our children are comfortable and relaxed – only then will they thrive and flourish. This book is not intended to provide information on how to change our children. It is focused on creating the type of environment that will allow our children to be authentically themselves, thereby enabling them to flourish.

Chapter 1

Sensory Needs

I am beginning with an exploration of sensory needs because, for our family, once we began to unpick all our individual sensory likes and dislikes, life became a lot easier. Having unique and individual sensory requirements is common to all autistic children (and adults), and creating a good sensory balance – reducing the intolerable and increasing the pleasurable – is paramount to creating a more emotionally regulated and happy person.

Life is full of sounds, smells, textures, colours and brightness. Each individual child will respond differently to differing stimuli. Each individual child will also experience how they feel inside their own bodies differently. Being autistic means that these sensory and bodily experiences may be intensely pleasurable and produce euphoric enjoyment or calmness, or they may be intensely painful resulting in deep and genuine distress. Some children may not recognize or respond to some external or bodily stimuli at all. A lot of autistic people are a mix of all of these.

In our family, we all have conflicting sensory likes and dislikes and we are even contradictory within ourselves. I like bombarding my senses with loud rock music, with a good vibrating bass line and strobe lighting, but place me in a shopping centre on a busy Saturday afternoon and I am reduced to a panic due to all the conflicting sounds fighting for my attention. The shopping centre brings me to the point of crisis by physically hurting my ears, whereas the rhythmic and repetitive patterns of particular songs suspend me in calmness. For me, listening to music when out and about enables me to access busier places.

It was observing my son's extreme sensory seeking when in distress that prompted me to consider that he may be autistic. He displayed strong sensory preferences from a very early age (suckling for long periods of time as a baby, smearing paint over himself rather than the paper as a toddler, stroking stinging nettles as an inquisitive pre-schooler), but it wasn't until he experienced full crisis and could no longer attend school that I managed to collate and begin to understand how his senses were experiencing the world.

In the first few weeks of leaving mainstream school my son was gripped by debilitating anxiety, responding to the trauma he sustained there from various restraints. This was before he had been diagnosed as autistic; his school could not accept that he might be autistic and so all 'management' of his 'behaviour' by them led to greater anxiety for him. He responded by simultaneously shutting down and 'hitting out'. He could not get dressed and opted for soft and fluffy onesies instead of day-to-day clothing. He could not wear shoes or socks or tolerate having his hair brushed. He either bounced around, over and on all the furniture, or screamed. At the peak of this crisis, he was having lengthy episodes of extreme distress several times a day, and it is what I observed him regularly doing in these 'meltdowns' that provided me with clues as to what he needed. In each episode, he was unstoppable – up-turning furniture, throwing ornaments, pouring flour from cupboards onto the floor, squirting liquids, turning on taps, unravelling reams of toilet roll and finally rolling around in all the mess. I eventually realized that when he began rolling around in the flour or water or sugar (or a mixture of all!) this was the point at which he began to calm down.

The majority of professionals around us at the time viewed his behaviour as manipulative and naughty. For them he was simply 'acting up' in order to avoid going to school. They advocated a firm no-nonsense approach, utilizing boundaries created by rewards and punishments. Experience taught me that reward charts and non-related consequences (such as loss of a toy) had no impact whatsoever. At the time, I did not know why, but I did know that that type of rigid behavioural system exacerbated the behaviour rather than quelled it. By looking beyond the behaviours and considering what needs particular actions were serving, I began to provide my son with opportunities to sensory seek before entering into any distress. I emptied whole bags of cheap flour onto the kitchen floor and built him mounds for his dinosaurs to explore. I recall him immediately preferring to smooth the flour with his skin, eventually leading to him repetitively swirling symmetrical patterns with his hands and then smearing the flour all over his face. In this situation, he had no need to avoid any unpleasurable task and was simply absorbed in tactile play.

I deliberately made time for sensory play each day and gradually he required less input. At present, he only requires a can of shaving foam to play with at bath time and his sensory needs are met. When his anxieties increase, then his sensory seeking in distress increases and we build more tactile play back into his daily routine.

Truly understanding our children's particular sensory requirements allows us to create an environment that is right for them and will allow their distress and anxieties to lessen. Some sensory input will need to be reduced, avoided or limited as it will be painfully intolerable for our children. Some people may argue that this is creating an unrealistic bubble of existence and not teaching our children to adapt to the outside world. I believe that the outside world should strive for inclusion and create more equality of accessibility for autistic people. While waiting for that to happen, I prefer not to place my children in tortuous situations with expectations that they cope and I choose instead to make their home life free from sensory distress. Everyone deserves an environment in which they rest and recuperate sufficiently.

Some sensory input will need to be increased to allow for self-regulation. This will most likely be activities that our children already seek out or find enjoyable. I view these types of sensory activities as therapeutically necessary and they can be built into play or daily life.

Analyzing your child's sensory requirements

Occupational therapists or good autism practitioners can offer sensory profiling services, but unfortunately, at present, regional areas vary greatly with regards to service provision and this option is therefore not available to every family.

There is lots of good and free information around sensory processing to be found on the internet. The Autism Education

Trust provides a Sensory Assessment Checklist, which is a useful tool for beginning to unpick your child's individual needs.

As you are investigating your child's sensory responses, consider whether they are avoiding certain sensations or seeking out certain sensory experiences. Most children will be both hyper(over)sensitive to some input, and will show this through distress (screaming at a toilet hand dryer may indicate auditory hypersensitivity for example), and hypo(under)sensitive to other input (indicative through a low pain response or deliberately seeking out stimuli). My son enjoys seeking out sour foods and splashing extremely cold water on himself, which combined with his love for hurling himself on the floor, has led me to conclude that he has some hyposensitivity to touch.

It is worth noting that an individual may present as having contradictory requirements, and in my experience this is extremely common. A person can be very sensitive to noise but at the same time enjoy seeking out noise-making experiences of their own creation! My eldest son is very hypersensitive to touch and dislikes hugs, and so on, but he does like a weighted backpack when leaving the house.

Activities and aids do not need to be complex or expensive to be successful – strategies to increase input usually are a lot of fun. For my son's weighted backpack, we haven't purchased a specifically weighted item (commercially produced vests, jackets and bags are available) but instead pack his favourite bag with jumpers until it's at a nice weight for him.

SENSORY PREFERENCES

Sensory area	Possible indicator (behaviour)		Suggested activity or aid	
	Avoids (hypersensitive)	Seeks (hyposensitive)	To limit sensory experience	To increase sensory experience
SOUNDS	Shows clear distress at specific noises: lawnmower, helicopter, hairdryer, vacuum cleaner. Covers own ears at particular times. Becomes over-aroused/'giddy' quickly in busy places. Complains that standard pitched voices are 'shouting'. Hears exceptionally well, including whispering, conversations at distance.	Likes self-selected noise-making: banging, singing, shouting. Enjoys loud music. Enjoys certain auditory sensations: whispering.	Provide ear plugs or ear defenders. Provide noise-cancelling headphones and MP3 player to 'block' out extraneous noise. Provide access to quiet space/ environment.	Play whispering games. Use music – both creating and listening. Make rainmakers, rice shakers, maracas.

VISUALS			
Complains of headaches.	Is drawn towards flashing or multi-coloured lights; strobe lighting, disco lights, traffic lights.	Use sunglasses, tinted glasses or light responsive glasses.	Play with torches and glo-sticks.
Shields eyes or squints at certain times.	Is mesmerized by quickly changing light patterns.	Maximize natural light.	Provide disco lightbulbs.
Seeks out darker spaces or shows preference for having curtains closed.		Remove any flickering lightbulbs or bright, fluorescent strip lighting.	Provide flashing toys: balls, Christmas spinners.
Shows distress when changing between differently lit environments – from inside to outside, for example.		Provide access to a dark, quiet and calm area.	Use colour-changing LED candles or projectors.
Has aversion to certain colours and patterns.		Keep decor neutral: plain walls (white, magnolia) with minimal pictures; plain patterned carpets and curtains.	Experiment with bath lights.
		Explore colour therapies – green is purported to be restful.	Explore colour and pattern preferences. Symmetrical patterns can be pleasurable and restful.

Sensory area	Possible indicator (behaviour)		Suggested activity or aid	
	Avoids (hypersensitive)	Seeks (hyposensitive)	To limit sensory experience	To increase sensory experience
SMELLS	Has gagging reflux reaction to certain smells. Shows distress around certain strong-smelling food types: blackcurrant juice, cheese. Covers nose and mouth at certain times. Refuses to walk past certain smells or runs away from particular smells such as cigarettes, vaping, car exhausts, coffee, car fresheners.	Habitually smells clothing from a young age – sleeves, cuffs, hems. Has a comforter that is also smelt from a young age – a particular shirt, vest, soft toy. Seeks out and enjoys favourite smells. These smells might not always be typically considered pleasant: books, dusty cushions.	Maximize air flow within immediate environment. Have a face mask, cloth or scarf to cover nose and mouth when needed. Soak tissue or face cloth with essential oil to mask unpleasant smells. Peppermint and lavender are useful. Minimize use of synthetic smells within the home. Consider cleaning and laundry products.	Have favourite smells accessible. Don't wash any of these without prior consent! (Yes, this includes the dog's head – my favourite smell!) Provide dried flowers/herbs – lavender sachets. Grow flowers and herbs in garden: rosemary, thyme, mint, coriander are all great plants for both touch and scent. Try essential oil burners.

ORAL			
Has an aversion to brushing teeth. Shows distress at mealtimes. Dislikes watching others eat or drink.	'Chews' drinks. Shows strong preference for suckling – thumb, finger – from birth. Suckling continues throughout childhood. Resists stopping breastfeeding/bottle feeding or using pacifier. Explores objects orally for a longer time than peers. 'Eats' unusual matter: stones, chalk, dust, mud, rabbits' poo. Reacts neutrally to sour or spicy flavours.	Explore alternative toothpastes: different flavours, non-flavoured. Provide soft brushes. Allow respite from distressing experiences.	Provide chewing gum. Give access to crunchy food textures such as apples, carrots, baguettes, rice cakes, breadsticks. Try different types of chewelry. Invent straw games: blowing paint through straws, blowing ping pong balls, blowing bubbles. Make fresh lemons or limes accessible for sucking.

Sensory area	Possible indicator (behaviour)		Suggested activity or aid	
	Avoids (hypersensitive)	Seeks (hyposensitive)	To limit sensory experience	To increase sensory experience
TOUCH	Resists and avoids light, affectionate touch such as hugs and pats. Is distressed by having hair brushed or nails clipped. Is distressed by having face (or other body parts) washed. Is distressed at wearing certain types of clothing. Is distressed by getting hands dirty or sticky and avoids messy play/baking. Avoids using full hand/palm for tactile activities such as art, baking, washing.	Seeks out multitude of textures. Has neutral pain response or may not notice cuts and bumps unless there is a visual prompt such as blood. Shows no response to nettle stings – may even seek out nettles to touch. Seeks out heavy physical contact such as wrestling. Enjoys stimulating skin via activities such as smearing body in liquids, extreme water splashing, rubbing against soft, fluffy surfaces.	Give lots of personal space. Ask permission to touch. Avoid light touch. Consider which clothing is preferable – cotton, fleece, baggy?	Provide lots of varying messy play activities: foam play, play dough, baking, water play, sand play, slime, squishy/squidgy balls. Explore whether massage might be useful. Provide different textures: smooth rugs, sequined cushions, spiky balls, bristles.

BODY – Vestibular	Avoids playground equipment that spins or rocks. Has a fear response to travelling up or down escalators/lifts. Can find walking up and down stairs frightening or difficult. May drop items regularly or walk into static objects. May struggle with some full body motor movements such as swimming, dancing, riding a bike.	Is extremely active and appears to be in constant movement. Is athletic and talented at physical exercise: running, climbing, gymnastics. Acts in an impulsive manner. Bounces on and off furniture. Explores the world from many and varied angles such as hanging upside down.	Provide playground opportunities at quieter times to enhance confidence. Consider seeking advice from an occupational therapist. Have lots of patience and recognize that your child may feel frustrated at times.	Invest in cheap home gym equipment. Pull-up bars that fit onto door frames might be useful (We have a treadmill and an exercise bike.) Explore accessible sports clubs. (Your local Scope or Mencap organization may have useful information.) Explore local authority grants for adapting your property. Charities such as the Family Fund may offer grants towards equipment. Offer active, physical games such as hide and seek. Pillow fights are also good. Visit playgrounds or outdoor gyms whenever possible.

Sensory area	Possible indicator (behaviour)		Suggested activity or aid	
	Avoids (hypersensitive)	Seeks (hyposensitive)	To limit sensory experience	To increase sensory experience
BODY – Proprioceptive	Avoids physical activities or sports. Avoids touching other people. Sits still (as opposed to being in constant movement – 'fidgety').	Has the appearance of being in constant motion. Walks loudly. Has a strong preference for sucking. Enjoys or seeks out firm, physical contact. Hugs in a robust way. Rolls, runs, slams against or on furniture. Bounces off walls – in a literal way. Is happy to wear tighter clothing: tights, knee-length socks,	Give lots of personal space. Consider how necessary it is to visit busy and crowded places. Explore physical activities which offer a gentler pace and exert no pressure on the body, such as yoga.	Offer lots of physical play: football, swimming, running, gymnastics, playgrounds and gym equipment. Consider investing in a weighted blanket or heavy duvet. Use wheat bags as weighted aids. Some people like to place them on their laps or around their shoulders. Explore home gym equipment. Peanut balls and resistance bands are good. Use large cuddly toys for squeezing. Make 'crash mats' from old sofa cushions. Invent games that involve deep pressure, such as arm wrestling. Explore quiet sessions at local trampoline or soft play centres. Provide opportunities for heavy household or gardening chores such as pushing a wheelbarrow or shopping trolley, digging, sweeping, washing floors. Create games that involve exercises such as push-ups, jumping jacks. Turn these into a competition to avoid any demand avoidance.

The PDA conundrum

Even with the most considered daily sensory equipment and activities in place, a child with extreme anxiety may view these provisions as demands to be avoided. In some situations, even bodily needs – such as sensory needs – place a demand on the child, leaving them in the complex situation of needing to use their body in a particular way but that bodily requirement then placing an internal demand on them. I have witnessed my children in acute distress because they could not overcome their internal resistance to needing the toilet, or getting out of the bath and drying themselves, while simultaneously desperately needing the toilet/to get out of the bath. This type of situation is truly heartbreaking as the intensity of their internal battles is not easily overcome. I only noticed a decrease in this specific type of bodily demand avoidance when their anxieties lessened holistically in all areas of their lives. And a good, daily sensory diet did contribute to this.

Autistic children (and adults) typically need a direct prompt to ensure that shared understanding of a strategy has been delivered; however, anxiety-based avoidance means that a direct approach can be perceived as a demand and subsequently this can trigger avoidance. With my son, if I suddenly proclaimed that every day at 10am we would go on the trampoline I can guarantee that this would not happen. Our children do like routine, but routine created by them and for them. Any sensory plan is more likely to be successful if our children can make autonomous choices – self-selection is probably the most useful strategy. In our house, we have small baskets of fiddle toys in all rooms, a peanut ball behind the sofa, a football goal in the hall, fluffy rugs on some floors, cheap shaving foam to hand in the bathroom and packets of chewing gum left in strategic places! All our walls are painted white and our carpets and curtains are plain with neutral colours. Occasionally my son may accept me getting the peanut ball out when I notice him slamming into the sofa; but mostly if I verbally suggest an activity, it is met with a 'NO!' I often offer sensory activities in the form of a game or a competition – we have a lot of wrestling matches or 'try to get out of this arm lock' scenarios as they apply a lot of deep pressure and help with increasing his proprioceptive input.

Sensory needs during crisis

It is also worth considering whether there are any sensory differences between calm moments and times of distress. If there are, it may be useful to tactically leave certain aids nearby for times of meltdown – if direct suggestions are made during meltdown, they are unlikely to be taken up. If meltdowns are destructive there might be a way to subtly divert attention to preferable sensory outlets. When I notice a meltdown beginning and it is not averted by other means then I bring out our crisis items. These suggestions may seem outrageous at first but for us they work by meeting my son's immediate physical needs while diverting him from more damaging or dangerous outlets. I deliberately leave out squeezy water bottles filled with water (this is preferable to having the shower or bath taps left on for an hour – but yes, I get very wet) and I ensure that cheap flour is to hand (with more expensive smearable products – my coffee and expensive cooking spices – hidden away) for him to roll in. The decor of our home is now specifically designed to withstand the necessary deluge with linoleum floors and stain-proof carpets.

When my children are in crisis I have noticed that all noise, apart from that which they produce, is highly intolerable and so over time I have learnt to reduce all the sound I produce in these situations. For some families, closing the curtains helps to reduce unwanted input. Some other children seek out very dark, cold and confined spaces – cupboards, wardrobes, and so on. I really believe that our children intrinsically know what they need to help alleviate their distress, but often society deems this as odd or unacceptable and so we are reluctant to assist. It is also exceptionally hard to remain objective enough to analyze behaviour when our children are in the midst of such distress; but, over time, patterns might emerge that are helpful in understanding what may help during future episodes of distress.

In the aftermath of our meltdowns, and while undertaking operation clean-up, I like to remember that sensory seeking is not a choice for our autistic children but a need and it is natural. Restricting the natural behaviour of our children is cruel and having to suppress these needs for the benefit of outside society is likely to create emotional trauma over a long period of time.

Age-appropriate activities

Over the years, I have encountered several professionals and educational provisions wanting to 'upgrade' my children's sensory strategies for ones which they consider to be more 'age-appropriate'.

When a professional says 'age appropriate', they are meaning age-appropriate for neurotypically developing children and young people. Autism, being a developmental condition, means that we develop at a pace that is unique to us. It seems rather ableist to decide what is developmentally appropriate for an autistic person by using non-autistic markers.

I imagine that a neurotypical professional might argue that by allowing a child to engage in age-inappropriate activities we are exposing them to harm, by exposing their vulnerability to the outside world. But this position is entrenched within the perspective that difference is bad and not to be respected. We have the right to be our true authentic selves and not to be disliked for this.

If a sensory strategy meets a need, is not harming anyone nor is it illegal, then it is appropriate.

Chapter 2

Daily Life

Anxiety

Anxiety is the overwhelming feature of daily life for children with PDA. The social world is not adapted for autistic thinkers and so navigation of complex social rules poses many difficulties. Repeated exposure to a world that is not easily navigated becomes frightening and scary. It is a natural response to want to avoid situations that consistently make us fearful. Constant exposure to an environment that is not adapted to meet the needs of an autistic child will create long-lasting anxiety that, if not reduced, will lead to complete avoidance of that particular environment.

Living with anxiety for a lengthy period of time can mean that, in the interests of internal preservation, a default response mechanism develops which views almost everything in life as a demand. Automatic responses deflect these 'demand attacks'. Answers to every direct question or instruction become 'NO!' Even if to be compliant would result in a pleasurable experience. Even if the demands are demands that a child has presented to themselves.

Children are resourceful and will develop many strategies that assist in avoiding environments that are threatening to them, and many strategies that will help them to control their internal fear.

All children are different and can develop many different ways of controlling their internal anxiety. Some control those closest to them (Mum or Dad), some control objects in their home or how tasks are executed. This can make daily life both challenging and frustrating for everyone within the family, and it may feel extremely restricting at times. But our experiences run alongside our autistic child, and whatever our feelings may be, they will be insignificant compared to the daily fear that our children have to live with. It is imperative that as parents we view controlling and avoidant behaviour in our children as manifestations of their anxiety. Behavioural-type approaches (rewards, punishments) will only exacerbate their anxiety and make daily life unbearable. Sticker charts and the like will never create positive change for a PDA child, because a sticker chart becomes the demand and since the chart content is focused on what a parent wants to change, they often demand the impossible from a child who is already operating within a state of high anxiety.

Before I focus on the specifics of day-to-day life, it is worth noting that the best approach is to help reduce your child's anxiety holistically – when your child's overall anxiety levels reduce, resistance around daily tasks also reduces. So, alongside the strategies that I advocate below, it is also worth considering the use of daily stress-relieving techniques such as grounding and guided meditation.

Demands and control

For my family, the combination of years of mainstream primary school attendance (with no adaptations in place to make life easier for an autistic child) and using sticker charts at home to enforce typical behavioural expectations led to overwhelming peak anxiety levels and shutdown within all areas of daily life. Every part of daily functioning became a demand, and everything was met with full avoidance – sleep, food, washing, dressing, going to school, going outside, seeing friends and family, playing, talking, drawing. Simultaneously, my son sought to control his anxiety by exerting control over innocuous tasks. As I was my son's main carer, it was always me that he sought out to assist him, and he, in turn – in order to control his anxiety – placed continuous demands on me. Striving for perfection became a big part of our lives as he sought perfection in the execution of most tasks. Opening bananas often escalated into long and stressful experiences because if I opened the first banana incorrectly (for example, if the stalk didn't snap well and mushed the top), then I would need to open banana after banana until the perfect banana emerged. No standard parenting technique offered any useful help during a banana episode – offering to slice the mush away was tantamount to declaring war. Parental firmness, such as my refusal to open any more bananas, would result in hours of him experiencing acute distress. The only strategy to such deep-seated perfection-seeking is to work alongside the child with patience and silence. Patience and silence are primary skills for a PDA parent. (And perhaps a sense of humour. It certainly didn't feel amusing for either of us at the time, but with hindsight I can feel some gratitude that I now have most excellent banana assessment and opening skills.)

During this time, my son developed many different approaches to task avoidance. As I write, I am conscious that it may read to some as if he cognitively pre-plans such avoidance in an effort to manipulate me as parent. Certainly, this has been suggested to me by several professionals. I firmly believe that no autistic child 'chooses' to continually avoid and resist daily functioning tasks. The energy that is involved in such resistance is phenomenal. It is not that my son 'won't' carry out a task, it is simply that he 'can't' – the anxiety has taken a firm hold. For example, he may want to get dressed in order to access something pleasant outside the home, but wanting to comply with this demand does not make the demand any easier to action. Instead of dressing, my son will roll around on the floor, declare that he cannot use his arms, pile sofa cushions on top of himself and declare he needs urgent help, throw his clothes onto high shelves and eventually work himself into a state of distress. Barking orders, issuing ultimatums and time limits or offering punishments only fuels the distress further. For an autistic child who does not experience acute anxiety, then a functional breakdown of a task into small, separate steps would be really useful. Unfortunately, for an autistic child with anxiety-based demand avoidance, such step-by-step flow charts can present the demand in a much more overwhelming way – one demand has now been broken down into many more demands. I have tried this functional approach and it mostly ended with a beautiful visual being torn into several hundred pieces – demands gone!

Reducing demands

When thinking about reducing anxiety holistically in your child's life, it can be beneficial to assess how demands in their day-to-day life can also be reduced. Does your child need to have a bath every day? Does your child have to say please and thank you to you? These types of expectations place a lot of demand anxiety on our children, and so relaxing our own parental expectations can be really beneficial to their mental health. Identify which parts of daily life are non-negotiable – for us it was teeth brushing, set bedtime, one learning task per day and one outside walk – and focus your energy on maintaining these. As anxiety gradually reduces, then more non-negotiables can be added. In the meantime, try and relax about the rest. At the beginning of our 'anxiety reduction journey' my son would only wear fluffy, animal-based onesies. I had to develop my own resilience techniques in order to ignore the sideways glances at my rather large dinosaur in Crocs. As his daily life gradually settled, we included an additional non-negotiable boundary around wearing 'outside clothes' when venturing out of the home.

As part of our demand reductions, I chose to not regulate snacks – even if this meant a snack being eaten as I was cooking tea. At the time where my son's anxiety was extremely high, he would seek out lots of sugar. Letting him eat sweets in an unregulated manner felt incredibly wrong for me, but I could see that it was somehow supporting his ability to emotionally self-regulate. The natural consequence for him choosing sugary snacks was my rigid enforcement of good teeth brushing. Using natural consequences instead of applying traditional reward/ punishment systems has meant that my son has developed his own self-moderation in a way that would never have happened if I had just 'told him' he must comply with my rules. He is now a healthy snacker, regularly choosing apples over sweets. Trusting my child to eventually make the right choices has been enlightening to me as a parent. I have learned that gently guiding decision making via the advocating of 'informed choices', rather than delivering direct instructions, has been the quickest way to reduce daily anxiety.

Screen time

An area in which it may be difficult to hand over all autonomy to our PDA children is 'screen time'. As parents, we are bombarded with advice from all sectors telling us that too much screen time is bad for our children: the blue light that radiates from handsets can disrupt sleep patterns, the child can be exposed to harmful content, reading skills will be impacted, and so on. But as parents to autistic children, we know how beneficial screen time can be – it can regulate mood by allowing our children to 'switch off' from the outside world. For a child who needs to exert control over their world in order to reduce their internal anxiety, time spent online can almost be seen as therapeutic. Combined with the autistic ability to hyper-focus (focus to the exclusion of all else) on tasks that are meaningful to them, time spent in online places such as *Minecraft* could be viewed as essential to their daily life. Personally, I do feel that our autistic children need a little more time in the digital/virtual world than their neurotypical peers might. Every family will have their own concept of how much screen time is too much. When my children were very young (primary school age), I over-regulated their screen time because I hadn't realized how essential it was for their decompressing of the day's events – autistic children do require much more time to relax after a day in school because they are utilizing far more processing energy than everyone else. Over-regulation in this area created many confrontations that were not necessary or conducive to helping my children reset.

Some parents like to negotiate time limits with their child and then reinforce these boundaries by setting timers or changing wifi passwords. PDA children will engage well with negotiating parts of their daily schedule as it allows them control; but, in practice, if an autistic child is in mid-hyper-flow when time-up is reinforced, then expect them to react passionately to the abruptness of the end. When in hyper-flow, a child's mind is fully committed to the experience in which they are engaged, and cutting through this flow – even when pre-arranged – will provide a severe jolt to their system. I have spent years trying to perfect my 'time's up' approach. Countdowns, such as giving warnings at decreasing intervals, increased my children's anxiety to the point of great panic. However, sitting alongside them in silence and then gently asking a question relating to the activity, slowly brought them back into household reality, enabling me to proceed to switching the device off.

My children self-regulate their screen time for themselves now. If their personal, non-negotiable tasks have been completed, then I am happy for them to judge how much digital time they need for themselves. How much time they dedicate to their tablets indicates to me how anxious they may be feeling – or how much more recovery from the day they may need. I have read some books around autism where parents are advised never to allow their children to emotionally regulate via their computer. I disagree – if our children can avoid heartbreaking meltdown by using screen time to create the space away from others that they need, then surely this is of benefit?

Routines

Autistic children thrive with having good daily routines. It encourages feelings of security in a world where social rules shift and unexpected events bring surprise. For an autistic child who is also demand avoidant, routines can also feel as if yet more demands are being made. Working with our children to make their own routines can be helpful as we are empowering our children and, in my experience, they make the right choices and for the right reasons if they are not having them imposed on them. I have observed both my children develop their own daily routines that are both meaningful and therapeutic for them. Taking a step back from filling their time around non-negotiable tasks has enabled them to create the correct activity/recuperation balance for themselves. This will allow them to become more independent in the future as they now actively understand what they need in their lives that will allow them to cope with more neurotypical challenges. For example, my eldest son requires the certainty of watching the same television programme in the morning and daily time sitting in the garden watching the birds. Not imposing a stricter routine on him enables him to manage his own energy expenditure, which in turn enables him to participate in more activities outside the home.

Toolkit for tough times

If using a negotiated approach does not make the execution of daily tasks easier for our PDA children, and the tasks are absolutely essential to maintaining a healthy and safe life, then there are a few ways in which we can help lessen the challenge for them.

These are the approaches that I save for use when I need them most – waiting in queues, maintaining hygiene, needing to use a direct instruction.

It takes a lot of effort to maintain an upbeat, genuine, not-too-happy persona, but I have noticed that, for my children, I need to maintain a constant temperament – one that is slightly upbeat but not too joyous, as any extreme display of emotion will add to their distress. As adults, we need to find constructive ways to release our own daily frustrations, which can be a huge task when the majority of our day is focused on caring for our children. I have very recently found that singing disguises my own annoyance and impatience and works so much better than shouting ever did. If a direct instruction is about to escape from your lips – sing it! Today I sang, 'Please take your muddy shoes off in the hall' in an operatic style (which built up gradually in sound so as not to startle the audience) and it was heeded.

When my boys were very small and attending mainstream school (pre-diagnosis), every morning was a fraught struggle to feed, wash and dress them. Our morning routine was only ever made easier when I acted out the part of Momma Bear (including crawling on all fours and talking in a growly voice) and herded my little bear cubs up the mountain (stairs) to the stream (bathroom) to wash the honey from their noses and brush their fur. Uniforms became disguises for the outside world so that strangers would not know that we were bears. This maintained their attendance throughout the majority of Key Stage 1. Key Stage 2 became trickier as this is when both of my children really began to struggle with the school environment. However, we persevered for as long as we could, and playing games such as 'Who Am I Thinking Of', '20 Questions' and 'I-Spy' during the journey to school certainly helped to distract and momentarily ease their anxiety. As my children have become older, I have adapted this use of distraction for the times when I can sense that anxiety is becoming overwhelming. Using whatever topic captivates them the most, I launch into quick-fire statistical-based quizzing or ordering games; for example, name your top five lizards, with five being your least favourite. Encouraging them to list backwards engages the mind in a more active manner – the mind has to start thinking and moves away from entering panic.

High-level anxiety can also present as needing always to be the best, be right, or to win. My youngest son can be really motivated by competition and there are times when I can harness this to engage him with a non-negotiable task such as getting dressed. I often line up clothes and then either say to him, 'I bet you can't put all those clothes on in less than 60 seconds' or 'I bet you can't get dressed quicker than the dog can'. In setting the parameters of the competition, I ensure that he is only competing with himself and not another person.

I am aware that there are professionals who consider the use of distraction techniques to be unhelpful in the long term, their argument being that we are not empowering our children's independence from us as parents, and we are not allowing our children the autonomy to address their own anxiety management. The problem is that professionals measure parents by their success at getting their children to school, in a clean and calm manner, and until the neurotypical world truly understands that our autistic and PDA children require respite and recuperation from anxiety-inducing situations in order to find that capability within themselves, then we are always going to try and ease our children's distress.

Life skills

There are many components to daily life that we take for granted if they do not present a challenge for us individually. Executive functioning skills, such as organizing ourselves and managing our time well, underpin our lives as adults and parents, but not every mind operates in the same way. Autistic thinkers and people living with chronic anxiety can find these types of planning tasks difficult or overwhelming. Abstract concepts such as how much time has passed, or monetary value, may also present as challenging.

An occupational therapist may be helpful in providing a functional analysis in order to prepare useful support strategies. There are also many visual aids that can be made easily at home – a plain wall clock can be annotated to show times for shower, meals, bedtime, and so on; but, with a child who becomes overwhelmed by demands, this approach may trigger distress. I have known some parents who have successfully helped to manage their children's time remotely via alarms or 'Alexa'-type technology because the demand is not delivered by a person. However, an alarm might startle a highly anxious child, which ultimately would only increase their overall anxiety.

I have by no means managed to erase all executive functioning challenges within our household. It would be both unreasonable and unrealistic to do so as an autistic thinker should not be expected to change their natural state of cognition. I have instead found some small ways to facilitate support in these areas so that their distress and anxiety are triggered less. I have a 'leaving the house' visual checklist pinned on the front door but never guide them to use it – that way the demand to use it has been removed. Likewise, I have made a key fob which lists items to pack in a schoolbag – this also just hangs from the bag zip with no prompt to use it from me.

I play time challenges with my children throughout the day. These can include asking them to just guess what the time is, guess when they consider a minute has passed, or challenging them to see how many star jumps they can do in a minute.

Aiding an understanding of monetary value is an ongoing project. I have one child who is frightened to spend any money for fear that he will have none left, and another child who has, on occasion, spent £60 on a virtual dinosaur and then deleted it the following day. I strongly believe that this is not a teachable concept but one that is gained through experience and so I pay them to complete chores. The chores are simple and suitable for their individual skills, and they do not receive any money, apart from birthday gifts, without having earned it. At times, this has meant creatively inventing a few more chores so that they can buy those essential in-game coins, but over time, their need to buy expensive items has diminished.

Chapter 3

Transitions and Change

In our home, anxiety reaches peak levels on leaving the house. Whatever time of day, wherever we are going, however well we have planned and prepared, the transition from entrance hall to through the door is laden with stress for everyone. I have adapted the physical hall space with expectation of this (daily) stress – the walls are white and plain, individual garments are organized into accessible compartments, furniture is nailed down (refer also to Chapter 6, When Things Go Wrong), there is a tray of chewing gum handy, visual reminders and, most importantly, chairs – for me to sit and wait and wait and wait!

Transitioning from one environment to another is hard. We are leaving our safe, calm(ish) space for a different one. The immediate environment outside the front door may be familiar, but our bodies still need to adjust to the differing light, temperature and sounds. This is a common experience for many autistic people. A functional occupational assessment may be beneficial. My eldest son was supported at one stage by an occupational therapist who gave very useful and practical advice on how to help his senses adjust to the abrupt change more easily – wearing sunglasses, ear defenders, a weighted backpack, taking a sachet of lavender to smell...

For PDA children there is the additional element of the 'fear of the unknown'. What if the neighbour's dog starts barking? What if a motorbike suddenly appears? What if a helicopter passes overhead? Combine this with not knowing exactly what will happen during the journey or what may or may not happen at the destination. Combine this also with the fear of expectation – what will I be expected to do when I am there? How many impossible demands will be placed on me? It becomes understandable and rational to subsequently avoid leaving the home.

When a child becomes regularly fearful of leaving the home it is distressing for everyone but most of all for them. It is frustrating not being able to enjoy life outside our safe space. Self-confidence gradually erodes as we perceive ourselves as failing after each attempt to leave doesn't happen.

My son was unable to leave the home for several months at one point. We were supported via mental health services, and by using a very low-pressure, graduated technique, improvements were gradually made. We began by just playing in the garden, which eventually progressed to small and local walks – literally, loops around the housing estate to 'judge' the prettiness of each garden. (Many apologies to those who overheard us rating your handiwork – whatever your 'score', you played an integral part in my son's development.) There are some professionals (usually non-mental health specialists) who believe in 'just getting on with it' and advocate physically handling a child into the new environment. This technique can be harmful as the child is flooded with stimuli in such a swift way that it is impossible for the child to process them, and this leads to neurological overload or shutdown.

Indicators that transitioning is difficult for your child

Signs that our children are anxious around transitioning may be subtle: sensory seeking may increase, stimming may increase, and needing to complete unconnected tasks may increase. Needing the toilet may happen frequently around transitioning time, although I am never sure whether this is a physiological symptom of anxiety or a purely avoidant strategy. It can be useful to discuss this with your child at a later stage as I have found that if toilet time is due to more pressing physical symptoms, becoming familiar with our bodily reactions can help us to control and understand the impulse – knowing that the physical symptoms will pass as our anxiety lessens is both empowering and reassuring.

I am often met with a plethora of 'what if' questions while attempting to leave the house with my children. 'What if the bus breaks down?' 'What if we get mugged?' 'What if there's a madman with a gun?' Some questions may seem ridiculous and far-fetched, but I answer each one with practical advice: 'We will catch another bus', 'We won't fight back and then we will phone the police', 'We will run and hide'. Through trial and error, I have discovered that by dismissing the questions with replies such as 'Don't be silly' only serves to increase their anxiety. By answering honestly and directly, in a matter-of-fact way, I am acknowledging their worries and moving forwards. This can also lead to some humorous exchanges as the scenario questions become more outrageous, which often then helps to dissipate the fear naturally.

Parent/carer temperament

Before my children were diagnosed with autism, and before I became aware of the 'demand avoidant' profile, I faced many people (professionals and friends alike) who advised me to use traditional reward/punishment strategies. We had daily sticker charts, rewards for completing tasks relating to getting ready, and family support workers who liked to spend a lot of time verbally admonishing my children in order for them to 'learn consequences'. I had one support worker tell me that my child was being manipulative and was purposefully escalating their behaviour in order to get rid of them. I attempted to explain that my son's 'behaviour' was a distress response, a panic attack. She didn't agree and we parted with that service soon afterwards.

It was noticeably clear that behavioural strategies did not work – there were many mornings where my son was dressed in his school uniform but just could not go through the door to leave.

I am ashamed to admit that, because of pressure to show that I was parenting well and did have boundaries in place, I resorted to using countdowns and firm words, with a firm tone. This only served to increase my son's distress, culminating in complete shutdown and school/life avoidance. I should have heeded my instincts.

The only strategy to be used with a child in distress is patience and silence. For an autistic and highly anxious child this is more pertinent because of the added necessity of requiring additional processing time.

An autistic thinker may not necessarily confirm that they have received a piece of verbal information – a parent may interpret this to mean that they have not heard or have not understood – which may lead to the parent re-issuing this information, resulting in some metaphorical fireworks occurring and an immediate increase in stress. Leaving lengthy periods of time in between delivering information (verbal or non-verbal) allows the demand to be managed in a calmer way. I try to remember that every piece of information I give during transition is received as a demand, and each demand stacks on the previous one until they are no longer manageable.

Executive functioning skills, such as time management and forward planning, are integral to transitioning out of the home. People with sustained anxiety often report that their executive functioning becomes impaired when they are managing high levels of stress (see also Chapter 2, Daily Life). I made the decision to support my children's organization and planning in order to remove a set of demands. Leaving the house already requires them to expend a lot of emotional energy and I personally feel that packing their bags and setting out their clothes enables them to focus on managing their internal anxiety. There will be an opportunity in the future to focus specifically on these skills and this will be when overall demand avoidance has lessened.

Even with a deliberate effort on my part to minimize the demands associated with leaving the house, my children can still become very distressed and in this situation the only option is to be present but in a silent capacity. Sitting down and stopping can reduce the pressures associated with transitioning outside. However, this can also be interpreted as waiting for them to be ready – a demand in itself. My go-to manoeuvre is housework – putting the dishes away allows me to manage my own stress feelings and also removes my presence as a demand. (On a side note – I wouldn't recommend using the vacuum cleaner unless your child finds noise cathartic.)

Humour can be a great strategy to employ, but the timing is crucial. Applying humour when anxieties are too high may increase anxiety even more. Visual humour seems to be well received in our home as there is no additional need to process language or tone of voice. My eldest son struggles with his weekly transition out of the house and into college. The peak moments of stress for him involve ablutions – moving into the bathroom from his bedroom to complete a set of hygiene demands can be particularly challenging for him. Letting him naturally design his own routine for this (within time parameters) has really helped, and so I am up and out of the bathroom early enough to ensure that his routine is not disrupted. What has proved more successful has been placing his clothes to wear in ridiculous places around his room – including 'dressing up' a stray soft toy or even the family dog. This little bit of silliness appears to provide him with a little light relief from his internal battling.

Change

Change is notoriously difficult to cope with as an autistic thinker. If it is a change that is happening 'to us' rather than 'with us', then the change can be perceived as frightening and unnecessary. For children with PDA, being in control is an effective strategy by which to stay safe. Having control taken away – through change – removes all sense of security and safety; who wouldn't react to that? This is why surprises (even surprises that are considered 'nice') can be extremely distressing to an autistic thinker or anxious mind.

Surprises

For my 40th birthday, my very lovely mum planned a wonderful day of treats for me – pampering followed by a birthday meal. Unfortunately, it was presented to me as a sudden surprise (on the morning of my birthday) and I just could not cope. Instead, I took myself off for a walk in the local woods and hid from everything relating to my birthday. I organize my own birthday activities now – a little dull perhaps but this at least enables me to cope with some minimal celebrating. The sudden introduction of something new – a surprise – can trigger startle responses, meaning that our systems prepare us to flee instead of recognizing a well-intentioned treat. Many would be able to re-compose themselves, but a person with high anxiety may very well respond by opposing or avoiding the surprise, as this is self-protection.

Knowing this did not, however, prevent me from attempting to redecorate my bathroom one Sunday morning, while both of my children were happily engrossed with their computers and unaware of my intentions. In my mind, I was seizing the opportunity and being decisive. I began by painting over the tiles with a grey paint, and it was the strong chemical smell of the paint that alerted them to this unannounced change. My youngest son decided that I was being inherently cruel to the old tiles by covering them up and launched a protest, which at first entailed protest signs being made and attached to the dog who had been co-opted as fellow comrade in arms. By the time I had completed one wall, my son was experiencing extreme distress and was demanding that I stop immediately. The time for calm negotiation had passed and I could only watch as my son used varying liquids (shampoo, toothpaste, soap, face cream) in an attempt to remove the offending paint. The bathroom resembled an explosion in a paint factory and it was weeks before I could engage my son in a useful discussion about how we could best solve the problem. We eventually chose a new colour together – which is what should have happened at the outset! This is why I now make a concerted effort to minimize household surprises – even birthday and Christmas presents are discussed. If I am making any changes to the home (such as new furniture), I will ensure that my children are accepting of the change by enlisting their help or ideas in some way, even if this is just glancing at a website or watching me measure up.

Preparing for change

Preparing for change with an autistic child typically includes a lot of forward planning such as advanced timetabling and visual support guides. An autistic child with extreme levels of anxiety (such as PDA) may struggle with having a plethora of advanced planning because with each planning stage the demand of compliance is raised – the pressure to follow the plan becomes too great to cope with. I have made many a parenting mistake by over-preparing for change, creating wonderful books detailing what we might expect at the optician's, dentist's and cinema, all of which were torn up because the pressure placed on my son to attend was simply too much. I now introduce change in the most casual way possible. If the change will be significant (attending a new activity), then I may start by drip-feeding small pieces of information months in advance: accidentally driving past a new venue because a 'wrong turn' was taken, followed by the suggestion that 'it looks interesting' for another time. This introduces a new concept with no immediate demand or expectation. Occasionally I might introduce change by allowing my son to overhear me chatting about it to another person, or by leaving visual information around the home in a way that it will be 'accidentally discovered'.

I have also had some success with introducing new environments by 'trailblazing' – visiting by myself and then reporting back with a positive experience. When we needed to move house, and there really was no flexibility in terms of trying again on another occasion, my eldest son acted as 'trailblazer' by visiting the new house with me and then re-creating the new house in *Minecraft* for my youngest son, who was finding the transition difficult. This gave my youngest son the opportunity to explore his new home within a virtual reality and from the comfort of the old home before the finality of moving day. Many specialist autism schools now provide immersive, virtual reality rooms for their pupils to explore new experiences within their known environment – such strategies help reduce anxiety by gradual and repeated exposure at a gentle pace, aiming for over-all anxiety reduction as a child becomes more acclimatized to the change. This can be a successful approach for many autistic children, both with and without anxiety; but for a child where demand avoidance is entrenched, each attempt at exposure may still be experienced as distressing.

When our family life was very, very small and consisted mainly of remaining inside and only welcoming trusted visitors (because my son was too traumatized to cope with more), we played a game that we called 'the left/right game'. This game involved placing my son in charge of directional decision mak-ing – each time we reached a junction, he would decide whether we would venture left, right or ahead. As well as alleviating boredom, this game allowed my son to expand his engagement with the outside world at a pace entirely set by him. This in turn allowed him to manage his anxiety effectively because he was in charge, and progress was quickly made as a result.

A note about managing expectations

If we plan in advance for change and we prepare our children in a way that they can best cope with, then we must also prepare for the occasions when plans fail in some way or are simply different in reality to our expectations. Disappointment is a dif-ficult emotion to manage and, for an autistic thinker, imagining alternative outcomes in order to mitigate disappointment is tricky. I try to openly discuss with my children how advertisements present perfection and I try to make jokes about the differences between what I thought I was buying and consumer reality. This usually ends with one of my children declaring that I have been 'scammed', but it means I can then use the concept of being 'scammed' to broach what may differ in actuality to the plans that we made.

Chapter 4

The Art of Negotiation and Communication

'Say what you mean!' my exasperated children have shouted at me, when I have let an idiom or metaphor slip out accidentally. It is amazing how many nonsensical phrases we have within language, often passing from generation to generation with little change. Some idioms are easy enough to translate but many require you to just know what they mean. An autistic thinker interprets language in a literal way. Tone, metaphor, analogy and idioms are confusing and without any logical meaning – unless you just know what they mean. I make a concerted effort to use very few, but occasionally I do happen to use a non-sensical phrase because it is just so ingrained within common English usage. 'Ooh, this will blow the cobwebs away,' I blurted out recently, referring to the windy weather. My youngest son was immediately outraged! 'What are you talking about? That makes no sense at all,' he replied, and I found myself trying my hardest to explain what I actually meant. 'Why couldn't you have just said that then?' came his immediate response. And there is no plausible answer because he is correct.

'I'm off to see a man about a dog' was said to my youngest son as a farewell greeting. Many questions followed, relating to what type of dog our visitor was going to get. Where will the dog be coming from? Did I think that it would be friendly with our dog?

'Don't worry, it's not the end of the world!' My eldest son would enter acute panic every single time that he overheard someone say this in passing. He would be terrified, and it took such a long time to convince him that it only meant that the matter being discussed wasn't considered to be important.

Idioms, metaphors and analogies need to be taught and explained for an autistic thinker to be able to join in the communication in an equal manner. Without explanation, many of these phrases will not only confuse but raise anxiety levels for our children. Not being able to understand what is being communicated to you is stressful – it could mean anything at all, it could be really bad, and how would you know if it was bad if you couldn't understand it in the first place?

Written communication can be equally as confusing. I personally struggle with news headlines. The reduction into key phrases seems to remove logical meaning for me and I often place alternative emphasis on words, which skews the original intended meaning. I struggle to attribute tone to emails or text messages, never knowing whether the author is being pleasant or sarcastic. Anxiety tells me that they may be being sarcastic, so then how do I phrase my response? I am very thankful for emojis, as I can place a lovely smile at the end of my message to demonstrate that I am not intending anything other than pleasantries.

And, while I struggle with tone in written communication, my eldest son struggles with attributing meaning to the tone of verbal communications. Is someone angry if they are not speaking in an overly jovial way? Is someone being sarcastic when they are being complimentary?

Communication is, of course, a two-way exchange. I do not think that it should just be up to an autistic person to adjust their understanding and delivery of communication to fit with non-autistic protocol. Being mindful and inclusive with how language and communication are phrased and delivered can make a big difference to the daily anxiety experienced by autistic thinkers, children and adults alike.

Communication and socializing

As adults, we may think that our gentle questioning is polite conversation, an innocent attempt to engage in friendly small talk, and demonstrates that we are interested in the person we are speaking to. Mainstream society teaches us to express a friendly interest in other people by asking questions. For someone who is experiencing high levels of anxiety, such questions immediately heighten anxiety further. Even a simple 'How are you today?' can trigger worry and panic – what is the hidden meaning to this question? As an autistic person, I am constantly analyzing what the real meaning behind a social question is because I have historically understood social conversation in an alternative way. Because implicit meaning in communication is not initially obvious to me, I find that I am always on heightened alert in order to spot some implicit meaning. I may ask my eldest son on a morning, 'How are you today?', and he will respond with, 'Why? What's happened? Is it bad?' His automatic response is one of anxiety – is he being asked this question because something terrible has happened in the world and I am trying to find out how he feels about this?

In my experience, all questions are demands because they expect an answer. Questions raise anxiety because there may be several different answers to give – how do you choose which answer is most appropriate or accurate? And by the time our minds have performed this full analytical process, another question may already have been directed towards us to fill the empty, conversational space. Like many forms of verbal communication, autistic people benefit from time to process, consider and plan an answer. This can effectively lower a lot of anxiety around verbal communication.

Questions that are predominantly for the purpose of making 'small talk' are met with regular suspicion in my home. Our autistic minds do not always see the benefit of conversation for no other reason than making conversation. For an autistic thinker, conversation has a specific purpose – to know what is happening in the day, to learn and educate ourselves, to have our immediate needs met. Is it really necessary to chat and pose questions just for the sake of doing so? While a neurotypical thinker may feel they are helping by engaging in conversation, an autistic thinker may not have the same desire to connect socially in this way. My youngest son likes a lot of thinking time. He likes to ponder his particular interests and can get quite irritated by me invading his thinking space by trying to engage him in unconnected chit-chat.

A good way to engage on a more 'social' level with an autistic/PDA child is to engage with their favourite interests. Whatever they are interested in, demonstrate that you are interested too. This doesn't always have to happen in a verbal way – play is a great opener to shared engagement. Our autistic children will be experts in the activities they are most passionate about, and we will (most likely) not be. This gives our children a natural advantage, as they can be in control of an activity or conversation because they are the experts and we are learning from them. Many adults feel uncomfortable with such a hierarchical switch, but it is not nice to feel powerless. No adult enjoys feeling powerless or not in control – it is frightening. Our children feel the same, and having the opportunity to be in charge of a communication exchange by demonstrating their superior knowledge or skills is empowering for them. Anxiety will be reduced and defensive responses to social communication will lessen. Plus, it can be fun. I have learned so much from my children and, even though I will never be able to match their superiority in some activities, it is always a positive experience.

Trigger words

As a parent, you will, most probably, already realize which words or phrases trigger an adverse reaction from your child. Aside from confusing idioms and overly descriptive metaphors, many autistic children find factually inaccurate statements difficult to bear. My children are amazing at retaining facts and strive for factual perfection. They expect my communication with them to uphold these standards. If I make a factual mistake, then I will be corrected. If I refer to a stool as a chair, for example, or shampoo as soap, then whatever information I am trying to pass on to them is lost because the focus has immediately redirected to correcting – in detail – my noun faux pas. Larger factual inaccuracies take much longer to move on from, with often greater consequences. Soon after receiving a diagnosis of autism, my son was offered a course of cognitive behavioural therapy via our local children's mental health services, with the intention of helping him to manage high levels of anxiety. Unfortunately, whoever had written the adapted 'child-friendly' content had not considered the communication needs of autistic thinkers. In an attempt to describe how anxiety is a natural response mechanism, they combined metaphor with incorrect historical references and compared feelings of anxiety with stone age people running away from dinosaurs. My children immediately seized on this error and the clinician was unable to move on from this to complete the full therapeutic session. Their entire recollection of the session focused on how dinosaurs and people never existed at the same time, and all potential therapeutic benefit was lost.

The word 'NO!'

It is exceedingly rare that I use the word 'NO' when interacting with my children. 'NO' is a powerful word. By asserting 'NO', we are seizing power and control over a situation, and children with high anxiety/PDA need to feel in control because not having control over internal anxiety is terrifying. Our PDA children may repeatedly say 'NO' to us throughout the day. Sometimes it feels as if their use of 'NO' is an automatic reflex response. However, if we, as adults, assert 'NO', then we are attacking their autonomy and placing them in a frightening position. An anxious person is unlikely to cope well with hearing 'NO'. It is more likely to trigger a power struggle, which serves to help no one. There are many alternative ways to say 'NO', without actually saying 'NO'. I am not advocating that we do not reinforce our non-negotiable boundaries or that we let our children do entirely as they please – I am suggesting that we (as the adults) consider how we phrase or approach answering in the negative.

I have found that autistic people have a natural tendency towards justice. It is not very just to exert control over another person, particularly without reason. The key is to enable our children to engage collaboratively in discussion with us, so that they do not feel as if 'things are being done to them'. Working to problem solve together can be a useful approach, with often positive results. For example, my son may want me to fund an upgrade to the latest online game. Instead of saying 'NO' directly, I may sit and work through my finances with him (in a visual and age-appropriate way) and then ask him to devise a way to achieve his goal. When my eldest son was determined to forge ahead with a plan that I personally felt he wasn't quite ready for, I designed a written questionnaire for him to answer so that we could arrive at the same conclusion together.

My children have a wonderful ability to consider people equal to one another and believe that no one person is intrinsically better than another. My understanding is that many autistic people share this world view – some clinicians suggest that non-recognition of hierarchical status is a diagnostic marker. There will be some people who view this as having a lack of respect for authority, but I truly believe that this is a positive quality. By viewing everyone as equal then it follows that our children do not naturally make a distinction between adults and children. My children and I certainly converse on a par with one another. There have been times when this style of mutual exchange has been judged as lax parenting by others, but I consider raising children to understand that their feelings and opinions are respected in the same way as an adult's only benefits communication as they trust that they will be listened to properly.

Instructions

It amazes me how much of my daily communication with others focuses around giving or receiving instructions. As parents, we must spend the majority of our time asking our children to do something or teaching them how to do something. Verbal instructions are really hard to process if you are autistic. I find both receiving and giving instructions ridiculously hard. When receiving them, my mind begins to slowly shut down. I manage to process the first couple of words and then any following words just jumble together. When I am trying to give verbal instructions, my words jumble themselves as I struggle with the order in which to present the information. Words that connect sentences together vanish – I blurt out loosely connected nouns. A response to 'Where have you hidden the biscuits?' will be something along the lines of 'Cupboard, pasta, right'. Written instructions can prove just as difficult for me. I love playing board games, but reading through the rules sends my mind into disarray and I usually resort to just making them up as best I can. The only instructions that I have ever found easy to use have been flat-pack instructions, specifically from IKEA, which are wonderfully clear and visual.

Combine alternative processing with high anxiety, relating to the expectation of following an instruction, and instructions become huge demands – demands to be avoided, creating so much stress that shutdown and/or meltdown is probably inevitable.

When my children are experiencing high levels of anxiety, the easiest demand to reduce is that of giving verbal instructions. Are instructions necessary to the situation? Can we, as adults, model the desired activity or behaviour instead? Can we use clear hand signals to replace verbal commands? Can we reduce the intrinsic anxiety in following commands or instructions by approaching the situation with humour?

There are times when I know that if I approach the situation with a standard request, anxiety-based refusal will set in. As mentioned in Chapter 2, Daily Life, presenting a request in a non-traditional way can really help to engage your PDA child with what you are trying to communicate. For example, the daily request of 'Can you brush your teeth now, please' is very often met with, silence, annoyance, delay, dramatics or opposition. 'Well, I was going to before you asked, but I'm not going to now.' On occasion (when I am not exhausted) I use mime and ask my children to guess what I am asking, followed by a very enthusiastic and ridiculous mime of whatever the request or instruction may be. If I manage to secure a smile or giggle, then the probability of them quickly complying with said request increases. Competitions can also prove to be useful – 'I bet that I can get dressed quicker than you!' However, if I use the same tactic repeatedly, then that in itself becomes a demand. Inevitably, my children always seem to work out that 'the game' has an ulterior motive and then they may feel 'tricked' into compliance. When this happens, their refusal will most likely increase because I have broken their trust – an autistic thinker does not like duplicity. My advice would be to use these types of strategies sparingly and not to rely on them too often.

Our children as experts

A consistent approach in communicating with our PDA children is to defer to their expertise. As mentioned previously, an autistic thinker is likely to value every person as equal, which lends itself very well to having our children demonstrate how to carry out a task properly – a request can always be reframed as 'I'm not very good at this, can you show me how I can do it better?' Not only does this help complete a task more quickly; it can also really boost a child's self-esteem, which may be struggling when life with anxiety renders most things more difficult to achieve.

Offering choice

When trying to engage and communicate with a person who is so anxious that their default position is to object or communicate an outright 'NO', offering choice (or options) may help to lessen some anxiety by placing them at the centre of decision making. If we are honest with ourselves, nobody likes to be told what to do – it makes us angry and cross as we want autonomous control over our own lives. It is a basic human right to be able to exercise our own free will (within the parameters of law). Our children feel this too, and often with a fierce passion for justice. While we may wish for our children to be a little more compliant – and certainly we do not wish for them to act unlawfully – it is to the benefit of society as a whole that our children develop assertive voices and are able to communicate their wishes and desires effectively. For this reason, I am a firm advocate of negotiation and choice-based decision making as a means to empowerment. It is sad, but unfortunately true, that autistic people are often discriminated against within society; but if we teach our children that they are listened to by us as parents and caregivers, then we are providing them with a strong platform of respect from the beginning.

The problem that I have encountered with applying choice-based decision making within my family is that having choice can be overwhelming and can mean more opportunity to say 'NO'. From a young person's perspective, choices are not actually choices if they have been proposed unilaterally by an adult. Sometimes it is more useful to ask our children to help solve the problem instead. My youngest son will only take our dog for a walk on particular routes; and if he is having a particularly anxious day, then all route suggestions I make will be objected to. In this situation, I simply let the matter rest and ask him to come up with a solution instead: the dog needs a walk, so how best can we achieve this? Mostly, this is an effective approach – on the occasions where this doesn't work, we just try again on a different day. In order to not raise anxiety further, I only offer limited suggestions or options – perhaps just two. Anxiety is a powerful state of being and having to make any choice or decision at all can often be just too demanding.

Communicating through a third 'object'

There may be periods of time where all direct communication with your child triggers distress for them. If our children's anxiety has been raised for a significant period or if our children have become overwhelmed – rendering direct communication difficult to process – then approaching communication in an indirect way can prove helpful. Some parents like to purposefully allow their children to overhear certain telephone calls or conversations with others in order to give their children the information they need but in a less challenging way. Visual communication can be left around the home as 'clues' for others to deliberately see but without the demand of having to do so or the expectation of having to provide a response. I have done this with leaflets for activities or information relating to change. Sometimes this has proved successful and at other times the leaflets have been torn to shreds.

There have been lots of occasions whereby I have appropriated a toy to 'speak' through. For my children, speaking through one of their much-loved soft toys has provided them with a wonderful mixture of humour and comfort. It can be difficult to process what you want to say when caught in an episode of anxiety, overload and distress, and using their comfort toys to communicate can really help everyone to relax and regain calmness. In our family, I regularly 'talk' through our dog. Our family dog regularly operates in the role of mediator, crisis responder and negotiator! (She is an exceptional animal – calm and well trained, meaning that she is safe for my children to be around when in distress.) I provide a specific tone of voice and accent for her and she quite often oversees the trickier discussions. I am aware that to an outsider this may appear somewhat unorthodox, but it works. It is a version of de-escalation. The dog can be cheeky, rude and authoritarian, and still garner a positive response from highly anxious children. A word of warning though: if this approach is utilized a lot (as it is for us), then you may find yourself speaking in the dog's voice to the postman, bus driver and passing pedestrian!

Chapter 5

Education

If your autistic/PDA child is happily attending mainstream school every day, then (in my experience) your experience is a minority one. From the stories I read on social media and the stories I swap with my autistic friends, it appears to be that – for many autistic children – school attendance and good mental health do not co-exist. The mainstream schooling system is traditionally a one-size-fits-all approach and this rigidity can make school attendance a very distressing experience for many autistic children. From continual sensory onslaught, to high-intensity social communication requirements, a mainstream school setting is about as far from autism inclusivity as you can get. This is an extremely general overview, and there are mainstream schools that have skill and expertise with creating autism-friendly environments. However, there are a multitude of autistic children who have been failed by the system. This is partly because their autistic needs were not identified soon enough, meaning that traumatic school experiences were acquired, and partly because anxiety-based avoidance is so rarely understood.

My children both began their education within the mainstream schooling system and without any diagnosis. At school, they both presented as clever, shy and reserved. They complied with requests and participated in activities – so I am told, although my children recount to me now that it was often a teaching assistant who completed their paintings or baking to bring home. But at home, after the school day, they would scream and scream for hours. As a conscientious parent, I would discuss my concerns at their distress with school, only to be told that there were no issues at school and so the problem must be 'at home'. (I am not sure how our particular school could have failed to notice instances of sensory seeking via paint smearing though – my child was literally blue on collection.)

Holding it together at school by either suppressing autistic authenticity or being gripped by pure terror (as my eldest son describes his primary school experience) can only last for so long. It is simply too exhausting to continue pretending that everything is okay when, in fact, nearly every part of the school day is tortuous.

My children could no longer continue with their daily school struggles at the transition into Key Stage 2 (age 7) and that is when 'school refusal' began. I don't like the phrase 'school refusal' because it implies that they have made a choice, a naughty choice. In actuality, they had become exhausted through exertion at having to work twice as hard as their non-autistic peers – exhausted by having to battle with extreme anxiety on a daily basis. They had no framework to help them communicate how they felt, so they communicated in the only way available to them – non-attendance.

School 'refusal'

School 'refusal' does not spontaneously occur. There are indicators of school-based anxiety prior to distress manifesting as non-attendance. A good school will listen to you as parents and begin to apply strategies to make school life more comfortable for your child.

Although school life was always a struggle for my children, they persisted with attending until it all became too much. For us, the early signs of struggle were almost imperceptible – very slight changes that only those close to us as a family would notice. There would be complaints of tummy aches and sickness which, although accompanied with extreme paleness, never progressed to vomiting. Eventually I noticed a pattern to these bouts of nausea and discovered that days of physical symptoms occurred on assembly days. A good school, with a good understanding of autism and anxiety, will make reasonable adjustments for your child as soon as a difficulty emerges. Having school permission to sit out of assembly (perhaps by having some library time instead) is not an unreasonable adjustment.

Unfortunately for us, my parental observations were deemed to be inaccurate and the mainstream school in question decided that it was more appropriate to insist on my son's assembly attendance by delegating him the task of holding the doors open while class after class of noisy children marched through. A rapid decline in my son's mental health happened soon after (for contextual information, he was aged ten at this point), and within weeks he was physically making himself sick, in front of school staff, so that he could spend assembly time in the toilet instead. It still makes me angry when I consider how many early indicators I raised with our school professionals, only to be told that they simply did not see any issues! The ingenuity displayed by my son at this time was amazing. I am so proud that he found ways to take the adjustments that he needed in order to protect himself.

Interestingly enough, both of my children displayed similar signs of struggle, not at the same time but at the same age. On transitioning from Key Stage 1 to Key Stage 2, both of my children verbalized that they felt bullied and picked on in the playground. Again, teaching staff that I spoke to about this told me that this was not the case and my children were absolutely fine in school.

With my youngest son, the signs of struggle were clearer as his physical reluctance to leave the home each school morning became stronger and stronger. As more professional intervention was administered, more distress responses were elicited.

Regardless of whether your child has an autism diagnosis or a PDA diagnosis, schools should listen to those caring for a child when signs of school distress begin. The earlier help is sought, and the earlier support is given, the greater the chances are of minimizing your child sustaining trauma. Early flexibility, on the part of the school, is crucial to avoid deeper distress occurring for your child. Do not wait for a child to be unable to step through the school gates, before considering support strategies. As a parent, if you feel that your child's school is unsupportive and is not actively listening to you, take swift and formal action. Write to the leadership team, demand meetings with special educational needs co-ordinators, write to the governors, speak with your GP, request referrals to mental health teams and educational psychologists.

Below is a list of strategies and adjustments that may be helpful in supporting an anxious and autistic child in maintaining school attendance. However, it is exceptionally easy for autistic children to sustain trauma in a mainstream school environment. If adjustments are not made to enable an autistic/anxious child to access school in a way that they can manage, then real and long-term distress can be inflicted.

Useful school-based strategies and adjustments are:

- Offering quieter entrances and exits, separate from the main herd of children.

- Offering flexible start and finish times (without penalties) to relieve pressure from home to school transition.

- Recording non-attendance with an authorized/medical mark. Legal proceedings are unlikely to help an autistic child to re-engage with attendance.

- Structuring quiet time into the school day and allowing the child to access an alternative to the typically noisy and crowded segments of the day (assembly, lunchtime, playtime, PE).

- Assigning a key person to meet and greet the child when entering the school building and to support with transition from home to school.

- Actively engaging with the child's main interests and allowing them to self-select activities relating to their interests at any point during their time in school. This will allow the child to self-regulate independently.

- Offering a quiet part of the school that the child can access at any time of the day in order to self-regulate. Some children may like a library environment, some children may like to run loops of an empty gym hall – create an option that meets the individual needs of that child.

- Applying for an education, health and care plan (EHCP). A child does not need to have a diagnosis in place to receive an assessment for one.

- Relaxing rules around uniforms. Many parts of traditional school uniform can be sensorially intolerable for an autistic child.

- Offering a reduced timetable.

- Not expecting immediate and quick progress. Viewing progress in terms of the individual child rather than the expectations of the school.

School behavioural policies and PDA

I am focusing on the mainstream schooling system because that is where the majority of PDA children will begin their education. If a child is not displaying clear autistic communication patterns across a variety of settings and early on in their life, then it is unlikely that an autistic child will receive a diagnosis until life begins to create major challenges. Without an early diagnosis, autistic and PDA children will be navigating a mainstream school with few (if any) adjustments. All mainstream schools will have clear behavioural policies and many of these will operate a 'positive behavioural strategy'. It sounds nice, doesn't it? The word 'positive' implies that the school is respectful and caring towards its pupils, aiming to work alongside more 'challenging' individuals.

Unfortunately, positive behaviour strategies are tools of social conditioning. Similar to the concept of 'reward charts', these strategies operate by rewarding what is considered to be 'good behaviour' and punishing what is deemed to be 'bad behaviour'. As parents of PDA children, we know that our children are not naughty – they communicate distress at not having their needs met or in response to intolerable environments – and so, positive behavioural strategies do nothing but create internal conflict for our children. A distress or anxiety response is not a choice that they have made, so offering a reward for stifling their communication is just downright inappropriate and discriminative. Additionally, a PDA child may really, really want to achieve a specific reward but the demand to do so creates such internal anxiety that it becomes impossible to comply. In my opinion, positive behaviour strategies are psychologically tortuous for all autistic/anxious/PDA children.

Positive behavioural strategies exist entirely to promote societal norms. Such systems are intrinsically designed for the majority – the neurotypical mind. Any individual with a neurodivergent mind will fall foul of these expectations because our minds are neurologically wired in an alternative way.

If we consider the specifics of a generic mainstream school's behavioural policy, then we can immediately recognize areas of difficulties for an autistic child:

Punishments are given for: late attendance, forgetting equipment, not wearing uniform correctly, not complying with requests and instructions, shouting out…

Our children are punished for executive functioning differences, anxiety-based avoidance and sensory differences. It all seems so very wrong and it is easy to see why our PDA children struggle so much in a mainstream schooling environment.

If your child is within the mainstream system and struggling, then the first person to approach is the designated special educational needs co-ordinator (SENCo). Request a copy of the school's SEN policy. Request that reasonable adjustments are put in place immediately. My eldest son, although he was treated appallingly in primary school, had an amazing SENCo once he had transferred to secondary school (Key Stage 3). This SENCo immediately protected my son from receiving punishments such as class detentions or reprimands for forgetting equipment. These are reasonable adjustments for any child experiencing acute anxiety – with or without diagnosis. (My son didn't receive a diagnosis until the age of 13.) I also think a lot of professionals do not fully understand the complexities of using praise as a reward for a PDA child. Even with the punishments removed for a pupil, rewarding children with praise (verbal or written) is still utilized. Direct praise, when given to a highly anxious individual, can create extreme anxiety and stress. It is a demand – to continue to perform in whatever manner the praise was given for. Yes, on that one occasion, a PDA child was able to perform in a way that pleased the observer. But that does not mean it was an easy action; it may have taken a lot of energy expenditure which would be difficult to repeat. Praise demands that the action be repeated. Praise also demands that the individual behave in a manner suited to the observer, rather than in a way that is comfortable for the autistic individual. Our children may therefore find praise difficult to process; instead, they need us to trust that they are decent human beings capable of making morally correct decisions in an autonomous way.

Some parents of PDA children like to allow their children to overhear praise said to a third party. In my personal experience, praise is accepted when overall anxiety is lessened. Receiving praise when in an acute state of anxiety will conflict greatly with an internal self-view and only serve to exacerbate anxiety further. Self-esteem in an anxious and autistic child is a complex issue. As parents, we are desperate to show them how much they are valued, and all parents want to praise their children. Children need to be able to recognize their own worth before they can accept the praise of others. If a child has been struggling for a length of time in a school environment, where their natural aptitude and skills are not valued in the same way as their neurotypical peers, then it follows that their own internal sense of self-worth will be low. At this point, it is necessary to consider what changes will need to be made to their school life.

Considering alternatives to mainstream schooling

I can recall my elation when I discovered that there were many different alternatives to mainstream education – it felt as if I had broken through into a secret part of society. There was such relief that I no longer had to try and mould my child to fit into such a rigid system. It felt as if there was some hope left, and perhaps my children would be able to enjoy a good education after all.

The types of education provision available do vary greatly from area to area and so I must warn that my experience relates only to our locality. Generally, however, there are six variations of educational environment or setting: mainstream, resourced, partnership, specialist, education other than at school (EOTAS) and elective home education (EHE).

Resourced schools have additional funding to meet a specific area of need (autism). Partnership schools have specialist bases within a mainstream school. Specialist schools offer specialist education exclusively for specific needs. EOTAS can refer to a parent who holds an education budget for their child and purchases specific tutoring or activities for their child. EHE refers to a parent who funds and sources their children's education themselves. These are broad descriptors and I would highly recommend contacting your own local authority to establish what is available, as a first port of call.

My children's journeys through the educational system, post-mainstream, have been as individual as they are themselves. Both of my children have required long periods of recovery at home, plus flexibility and creativity (on the part of our local authority). We have not found one perfect school match and have had to measure progress via their happiness and well-being, rather than through qualifications.

To write about all the mistakes that were made, and all the wrong decisions taken, would not be fair on my children or the educational professionals involved. Maintaining my children's engagement with learning is a long-term way of life for us, not a 'quick fix'. At times, it has felt that the professionals and I were exploring uncharted territory together – experimenting with possibilities and reflecting on any small achievement. At other times, it has felt as if I have been the lone person advocating for what my children need amid a throng of parental blame.

The most successful approaches to retaining my children's desire and ability to learn are those that are child-led. Initially, recuperation was key – giving them the time to physically recover from the exhaustion of trying to fit into a system that would not bend in any way to help or accommodate them. Only then could we progress to discussing what they wanted to learn or achieve through education.

My mantra throughout has been: school is not compulsory, but our minds need to learn.

I personally feel that how recuperation is supported is crucial for future re-engagement with more formal learning. My eldest son, for example, remained on his mainstream school roll (with an authorized leave of absence) until next steps were agreed on and, more importantly, were able to be undertaken by my son. He wanted to pursue academic qualifications and was able to do so via a very bespoke package of education, delivered in an outdoors space where he felt safe and happy. He achieved his GCSEs without having to put one foot into a school environment.

The need for recuperation was not considered at all by the professionals 'supporting' my youngest son. Staff persistently attempted to retain physical school attendance and ultimately considered pursuing legal action against me as parent. At this point I had no choice but to de-register my son from mainstream school and electively educate him at home until his needs were fully assessed and understood. I applied myself, in my capacity as a parent, for an education, health and care needs assessment and was successful.

Having an EHCP is necessary to access more specialist schools or have the local authority oversee a more alternative package of education. Never believe any professional who tells you: a) parents cannot apply for an assessment for their child themselves; b) your child *must* have a diagnosis (the legal threshold for acquiring an assessment is that your child *may* have 'additional needs') in order to apply; c) your child must be attending a school. None of this is true and I secured an EHCP for my youngest son despite all of the above.

There are many sources of free and easily accessible information relating to applying for an EHCP. At first, the process may seem daunting, but an EHCP can prove a useful tool in securing support that is individually tailored to your child. Professionals may wish to offer generic solutions, but each autistic person requires their individuality to be considered, and it is through recognizing an autistic person's individuality that trust (in accessing a learning environment) will be rebuilt.

A lot of our initial home education was therapeutic – sensory play – in order to support his recuperation. This eventually progressed to indirect learning, and then interest-led learning.

Education at home

My children have received their education at home for a significant period of time. I have worked with some wonderfully creative professionals and I have worked with some rigid, disciplinarians. I can say with confidence that creative, flexible and bespoke strategies offer the greatest chance of success in terms of increasing a child's mental well-being and engagement with learning.

Good mental health and emotional well-being are the priorities for your child. No child can effectively participate in any kind of education until they are receptive.

The immediate fall-out from long-term school anxiety may be increased periods of distress. We navigated our way through this distressing time by using play – sensory/messy play, small-world play, board games, hide and seek...

As the daily distress lessened, we were able to include activities such as reading, baking and painting. This then naturally progressed to applying incidental learning techniques. If my son was drawing, then I would (with permission) draw alongside and then gently bring in some discussion around what we were drawing. If we were playing with bubbles, then I might gently include some scientific information.

It took approximately two years for us to create a solid routine of having a dedicated, morning 'learning time'. This was achieved by my 'teaching' being led entirely by my son's interests at the time. When he was highly focused on Pokémon, we used his Pokémon characters as maths aids to weigh and measure. We spent time outdoors searching for insects ('grass-type' Pokémon) and kept a tank of tadpoles to monitor their 'evolution'.

When attachment to devices has been high (virtual worlds and electrical devices are wonderful for enabling a child to be in control), I have adapted to encourage learning from within these platforms. *Minecraft* is amazing for exploring area, perimeter and volume. It is also great for geological exploration and creating historical architecture!

My son often verbalizes to me that he does not recognize the point of learning subjects if they do not relate to his real-world experience. As an adult, I can see his point – the only time I have had to recall certain parts of my education has been in order to teach them to my children. However, you never know what interest may be sparked by presenting something different, and for that reason I like to vary their exposure to subject matter. I do this in a very indirect way – I might stick a random, educational poster up on the kitchen door, without verbally directing any attention to it. I might put a documentary on while I am making tea – this usually captures interest sufficiently for them to wander in and tentatively watch from the side.

Fractions have been a particularly contentious subject for my youngest son – what is the point? In this situation, I have found that creating practical and physical situations is more likely to engage his interest – cake division always works well!

Allowing my son to showcase his expertise over mine has been integral in allowing him to recognize and have confidence in his own abilities. My son is good at mental arithmetic, whereas I have to write sums on a piece of paper and apply the traditional column method of addition, multiplication, and so on. Whenever we are practising these types of maths skills we 'compete' to see who reaches the answer first (and it is always him). From my experience, however, these comparisons must be genuine – if I were to fake not being as skilled as him in an area, then he would become very distressed by my lie.

Harnessing your child's natural skills and interests is paramount in retaining their engagement with learning.

All autistic individuals are unique; we all have our own particular strengths and weaknesses. Some autism professionals like to refer to this as having a 'spiky profile'. It can be useful to visually map out what these are for your child. If possible, collaborate with your child as it is always insightful to discover what they really think and feel about what they find easy or difficult. (And very often it is different from the conclusions made by the adults around them.)

Talking Mats offer great ways to unpick complex issues and provide alternative ways of communication other than speech. Essentially, Talking Mats are a communication tool whereby direct questions are posed and a set of suggested, possible answers is given alongside them. The person using the Talking Mat moves the answers into relevant columns (Yes/No/Maybe) to indicate their thoughts and feelings around the discussion topic.

It is empowering for any child to have their opinions considered. For a PDA child, giving them control is crucial for their progression. And understanding what skills and experiences they consider as positive allows us, as adults, to tailor their learning experience into a more pleasant and accessible one.

Finding a learning environment that your child will thrive in

There is no easy answer and no perfect school placement. Sourcing the best place for our PDA children to access learning is a journey and I often hear stories of children changing several placements before finding a good match for their individual needs. One school may be perfect for one PDA child but not able to meet the needs of another PDA child. This is worth considering when sourcing more specialist-type placements.

Each child is an individual and so we cannot base potential success of a placement on another family's experience. However, the ability of a school to adapt to the individual needs of each child is an excellent indicator of how well they may meet your child's needs. A placement that speaks positively about creating bespoke plans and can offer flexibility over time is more likely to meet the needs of an autistic child with significant anxiety.

Many schools offer physical environments that are of benefit to autistic pupils, such as sensory rooms, gardens, quiet areas, assistive technology and good playground equipment. I recall being drawn to these schools because I thought that good equipment was synonymous with good understanding. Unfortunately, this is not always the case and I have experienced appalling understanding of autism at the flashiest of specialist schools. For me, it is much more important to consider the ethos of the school – does the school wish to 'treat' autism and train children to fit into the outside world, or does the school treat each pupil with respect and work on building confidence and self-esteem? It is worth considering that alongside selecting an environment for your child to potentially learn in, you are also selecting a team of professionals with whom you will have to meet on a regular basis and discuss your child's progress. Consider if the professional view of progress is a realistic one. Transition into any new environment for an anxious and autistic child will be a gradual process. Consider which professionals truly understand this – who has the knowledge, experience and outlook to be able to support your child best? In my experience, professional individuals who can work in a creative and flexible way are the ones who help my children to succeed.

Our children's pathway through education will be vastly different from that of their neurotypical peers and it is crucial that we measure progress according to our own child and not against the progress of others. But most of all, we must be child-focused. We all have hopes, dreams and aspirations and there are many different ways to achieve these – mainstream schooling is not the only route.

Chapter 6

When Things Go Wrong: Crisis and Distress

When our children are in distress it is heartbreaking. It is heartbreaking for us, as parents and carers to observe, as it can often feel that we cannot do anything to ease their distress. It is even more distressing for our children who are experiencing crisis – it is both overwhelming and frightening for them. There are many words that professionals use to describe such autistic experience – crisis, distress, meltdown, shutdown – and whichever word is used, we must remember that these events do not happen by choice. An autistic child or adult does not have control over such distress responses. Meltdowns/shutdowns/distress happen as a result of becoming neurologically overloaded, due to specific needs not being met.

What might crisis look like to an observer?

A child may shut down and retreat from their usual pattern of daily life. They may spend more time in solitude or engaged in solitary activities where they focus all their attention on, for example, reading, drawing, computer games. They may be so intensely focused on an activity, for an extended period, that they neglect daily functioning tasks such as eating and washing.

Speaking or communicating in their usual way may be impacted. My eldest son, who has an extensive vocabulary and is typically articulate, is unable to communicate with spoken language when experiencing distress and instead utilizes sounds and gestures to communicate at this time.

Communication towards immediate loved ones may appear 'rude' or 'antagonistic'. This communication is an expression of anxiety and representative of their internal distress rather than a considered insult towards others.

Some children may engage in activities that are considered as 'self-harming' – 'hateful' language towards themselves, verbalizing a desire to hurt themselves or even to kill themselves. Some children may hit themselves or self-strangulate. Some children may cut themselves.

Some children may become aggressive towards those immediately around them, perhaps hitting out or throwing objects. Others may become destructive towards property or their immediate environment.

A lot of PDA children may experience all of these. I think that there is a media tendency to focus on PDA children whose episodes of being overwhelmed manifest in destruction and aggression and this is to the detriment to all autistic people. It plays into the stereotype that autistic people are unpredictable and dangerous, which is just not so. All of the behaviours detailed above are manifestations of neurological overload. The more inclusive society can become for PDA children, the less frequently these manifestations of overload will occur.

For my family, periods of crisis or distress happen when my children have been either 'coping' for too long in an environment that hasn't been designed for their specific needs, or they have been 'encouraged' to develop at a pace determined by others.

If an environment is not designed from the outset for an autistic child's way of being, then more time spent in that environment is to the detriment of the child. Some children express environmental discomfort in a way that professionals can understand immediately, but there are many children who either express this discomfort in a way that isn't interpreted well by professionals or who manage to tolerate the discomfort (possibly for lengthy periods of time) until they can no longer cope. In the adult autistic community, we talk about 'burnout' – the concept of struggling along, in neurotypical environments, until the toll of doing so becomes too much to bear. Autistic children suffer from burnout too. As adults, we recognize burnout as debilitating and take appropriate respite to mitigate this. The world has become more accommodating to adults practising necessary self-care, yet it is less acceptable for this to be applied to children. We expect children to have endless energy, resources and resilience, and we very often struggle to understand that, in the wrong environment, an autistic child may need to expend twice as much energy (due to processing) than a neurotypical peer. This is clearly exhausting and unsustainable.

Developmental progress is routinely monitored throughout childhood – by parents, by school, by health workers – and always measured against neurotypical development. An autism/PDA diagnosis helps professionals to understand why our PDA child diverges from this developmental standard but doesn't always help professionals to understand that progress should be at a pace that is comfortable for each individual child. Our autistic/PDA children develop and progress along their own timeline. Forcing progress or comparing progress to that of other children is not only unwise, but potentially very harmful, as placing unobtainable expectations on our children is tantamount to abuse. In my experience, placing demands on our PDA children to progress in line with the expectations of other people is the swiftest way to full-blown crisis, and that is cruel. We need to engage with our children and understand that progress occurs when their needs are met and they are ready. So many PDA children are let down by a system that wants to set out clear goals of achievement, only to attribute lack of progress to the child's family when the child does not achieve this. Pushing a child to conform to a set concept of progression, when neurologically this is impossible to achieve, causes neurological overload and mental health crisis.

As a parent to two autistic children myself, I recognize that supporting our children through distress can be unbelievably hard for us – emotionally, physically and financially. In supporting my children through several episodes of crisis, I have lost friends, relationships, jobs and my home. I have spent my savings on obtaining assessments, reports and legal advice. I have been exhausted for a long time. As I begin to share approaches that have been useful during such difficult periods, I think it is important to reiterate that however hard it is for us, it is ten times harder for our children. The core motivation for sharing our experience is to acknowledge the trauma that can occur for our children and how crucial it is to always remain focused on our child's needs – even when we are feeling under pressure. Periods of distress do not last forever, but mismanagement (unwittingly or from external pressure) can extend these periods and make them more painful for our children.

Useful mindsets for parents and carers

As parents and carers, when our children are experiencing periods of distress, it can feel as if our entire family is crumbling around us. We are emotionally connected to our children; it would be very strange if we weren't. When our children are hurting, we are hurting too. We want to be able to comfort them and make everything quickly better. Or we might be fraught after a sustained period of supporting our children's extended distress. These are normal parenting emotions to feel but, in my experience, they are not helpful support strategies. I often think that in order to support a PDA child in distress, one must become as objective amid crisis as possible. This is notoriously hard but does become easier over time. Imagine yourself crying uncontrollably in the GP surgery and then the doctor begins to cry uncontrollably too – distress escalates further and as a patient it is terrifying to have the person you are relying on for help be unable to help you because they are too upset.

Accessing parent/carer autism and PDA support groups was my lifeline in the early days of recognizing PDA as a part of my children's autism profile. I recall the many times I posted status updates in the middle of crisis and was given unwavering support – not judgement – plus a plethora of useful strategies and advice. A good parent/carer support group or network will be worth several expensive, professional reports. These groups are our safe spaces, and using them to share our thoughts will enable us to be the support our children need.

There really is no immediate quick fix that halts an episode of distress for your child. Early support can help, and I will discuss how best to identify these moments later on. But when distress has taken full hold of our children, patience and time are likely to be the only useful tools. Of course, we can alter the immediate environment to make it safer or more comfortable for our child; but, more often than not, the most useful assistance that we can offer our child is silently and calmly being present. This does not have to be immediately next to them (my children find it hard having anyone near them), but by just sitting (silently) out of sight we are demonstrating our commitment to them and our unwavering support. By not reacting to how their distress is presenting itself (within the realms of safety), it may feel as if we are acting in an uncompassionate manner, but we are giving them the space and security to eventually come through the crisis. One brilliant piece of information that was given to me is that after crisis has seemingly passed, neurologically, our brains are still operating in that state for 90 minutes afterwards. I wish I had known this years ago as there must have been countless times where I unknowingly 'restarted' distress for my children by encouraging them to do something their neurology was not yet ready for.

Crisis support – how to adapt

It is a cliché, but it is also true: in order to take care of our PDA children effectively, we must ensure that we are also taking good care of ourselves. Our mood, as parents and carers, will impact on our children and our own ability to support them in times of distress. If we are riddled with anxiety, then this is likely to add to their anxiety too. I am not saying that our emotional state has 'caused' our children's neurological difference – this is impossible – neurology is neurology. However, if our moods are inconsistent for a length of time or our mental health has begun to impact on our daily functioning, this can begin to impact on our children – whether they are autistic or not.

I have found that my children need a steady, consistent mood presentation from me, and this includes moments of excitement and joy. I recall a celebration whereby I brought home cake and Prosecco to share with friends and family. My children were as anxious with this very natural demonstration of happiness as if I had been crying in distress. It is unrealistic to remove all emotion from our day-to-day life; but if there are major changes to my usual demeanour, then I try my best to explain why. Some families like to display mood boards in their home in order to visually and clearly show how members are feeling – this leads to less anxiety and uncertainty over why Mum or Dad is singing or laughing.

As parents to autistic children, we are likely to be inundated with paperwork, meetings, appointments and telephone calls relating to our children's 'identified needs'. It feels like having a full-time job. The systems that support children with special educational needs are bureaucratic and there will be some people who can manage well with this level of administration, but for a lot of parents it can become overwhelming. This is where support groups and charities can be invaluable. It can be useful to connect with an advocacy-type service or charities that specialize in autism and PDA. They can help with advice and completing forms.

Practising regular self-care is as crucial as attending every scheduled SEN appointment. However you choose to take time for yourself, try to do this regularly. There have been times when I have laughed in response to this suggestion, especially when it was made by someone with no experience of PDA. Trying to find this time can be impossible, especially where sleep patterns in our children have been disturbed by anxiety, and especially during periods of crisis.

Crisis self-care is all about taking what you can, when you can, in the simplest way possible. It may involve sleeping on the floor next to your child because that is the only way you will obtain any sleep. It may mean negotiating additional screen time for your child to allow some exercise for yourself. Do not feel guilty about these adaptations, and do not make comparisons with your parenting and other parenting styles (especially that of parents of neurotypical children). The purpose of crisis self-care is to function enough to survive. Crisis does pass, and there will be opportunities to re-evaluate later.

Safeguarding

Every child communicates their distress differently, so it follows that any adaptations we need to make (to our home) to ensure our children's safety during episodes of distress will also need to be individualized.

Below is a short list of quick, easy and practical suggestions:

- Home safe for storing key documents.

- Locked medical box for storing medicines.

- Locked storage box for storing sharp implements (knives, scissors, razors, DIY tools).

- Wicker or rattan furniture.

- Window locks and window restrictors.

- Lockable technology cupboard.

- Television guard screen.

- Window film.

- Plastic crockery and tin mugs.

- Storage for any precious ornaments or pictures.

- Door and window alarms.

- Personal bag (waist bag, joggers' pouch) for ensuring essential items remain with the adult (keys, phone).

Some families are able to dedicate spaces within their home for de-escalation and calming. It may be useful to speak with an occupational therapist regarding such spaces in order to ensure they meet your child's individual likes and dislikes. My eldest son seeks out small, dark and cold spaces when he is in distress, but my youngest son needs to feel able to move freely around from room to room. Your child is likely to know what they need themselves, and so observing what environment or input they seek out for themselves when in distress will be the best guide for adapting your home to suit their needs.

Using an analytical approach

Working out patterns to our children's distress responses can be helpful in both understanding their needs and knowing what we can do best to help.

Most professionals advocate using a diary to note changes in distress levels over a length of time. As a parent myself, I know that this can feel like a massive undertaking. We are supporting our children directly and continuously, and having to make time to complete yet more 'paperwork' can feel pointless and frustrating. Make any diary you keep as simple as possible. Use charts and tables with coded annotations instead of writing out lengthy descriptions. Professionals look for key markers when monitoring distress – frequency, duration and intensity – so include these in any record keeping you undertake. Frequency refers to how often episodes of distress are occurring. Duration refers to how long each episode lasts for (and I would include recovery time here too). Intensity refers to how distress is communicated, which can range from crying, shouting and swearing to self-harm, destruction and suicidal ideation. It is useful to note what you, as observer, believe the trigger to be. In my experience, there are always two parts to the 'trigger'. The first is the immediate trigger, which is responsible for 'setting off' an episode of distress. For us, this can often be unsymmetrical shoes or a two-way communication misunderstanding. The second part to the 'trigger' is the wider context of current life for your child, and this may very well be something you, as parent, have no idea about. Are they struggling with an environment, communication with a particular person, adapting to a new (possibly small) change, having too many demands placed on them? Triggers are likely to be combinations of many, separate issues. My eldest son has been able to explain to me that distress doesn't begin at the point at which he visibly becomes distressed. It occurs much earlier and so the immediate trigger is often the point at which management of internal distress is no longer possible.

My children have developed insight into how and when life becomes intolerable for them and this has really helped us to help one another through crisis. It has taken several years to reach this point. By using a combination of my observing how their communication changes at the beginning of crisis and discussing this with them (Talking Mats are a great resource to use when needing to unpick issues with autistic thinkers), we have managed to identify the really early signs of distress approaching. These signs can include pacing, swearing, rocking, silence, thumb-sucking, blaming, disturbed sleep patterns, seeking out isolation, irritation.

Once early indicators of distress have been identified, then it follows to consider what types of assistive strategies may be helpful to introduce at this early stage. My youngest son needs verbal silence from me but also some high-level sensory input. My eldest son benefits from using early grounding techniques, such as searching for details in his immediate environment.

By grounding, I mean engaging the anxious mind in rational or logical thought. When in panic mode, our thinking can become stuck in loops of worry, making it difficult to process any more types of information. Focusing on small details immediately around us can guide our thought patterns back into more rational ones. The possibilities are many and varied: looking for insects, looking at the veins in a leaf, counting our footsteps, examining the thread detail in our sleeve. My eldest son has a formula: point out five things you can see, four things you can hear, three things you can smell, two things you can touch, one small thing. Of course, this will not be helpful if it is a sensory trigger that is causing distress, such as the smell of fruit juice. This method has proved most helpful for us when in busy crowds – for example, in shops.

Generally, autistic children need silence and calm around them when they are experiencing acute distress. Communication and processing communication will be especially hard at this time and often the most helpful approach as an observer is just to be silently alongside them. Any communication with children in distress should be brief and clear.

Allow your child a good length of recovery after distress has been experienced. Even after the outward signs of distress have dissipated, your child will still be feeling some level of internal distress and any extraneous and unnecessary external stimulation could very easily overwhelm them. Recuperation time is absolutely necessary – ideally in a quiet and safe space with perhaps a drink and something sugary. In my experience, recovery from such crisis is akin to recovery from shock. Thought patterns may be unclear, and the physical body may be providing a physiological response such as shivering.

Once these shock-like symptoms have begun to pass, our children may start to feel upset, or perhaps even guilty for any actions that may have occurred during their distress. My children often explain that they can feel self-loathing and depression following a significant episode of distress. At this juncture, I remove as many external demands as possible. Any immediate plans to leave the home are rescheduled, any decision making is postponed or taken by me, homework is postponed, and unnecessary ablutions are also deferred.

When my children are able to communicate again in their usual ways, I try to 'debrief' with them. There is never any blame given for behaviour that happens in distress, because I accept that they have become too overwhelmed to control what is happening. I reassure them that we will work together to fix anything that has been broken and I offer my own apologies for anything I may have done wrong or not handled in the best way. Never punish an autistic child for something that they said or did during crisis or distress. Their neurology was overloaded and there was no intention behind their actions.

Natural consequences can be useful in addressing some issues. For example, technology is often a common target for destruction during crisis but is too expensive to replace regularly. It can be argued that technology is crucial to autistic children as communication aids and emotional regulation, so I am not advocating that all their technology is removed or not replaced. However, it may be possible to only replace the essentials, to allow for some natural consequences – a favourite game no longer being in playable use, for example.

Emergency services

There have been times when other professionals have had to assist in keeping my children safe when in distress. Every incident that has involved school staff, paramedics or police officers has been a unique experience, with the outcome and trauma sustained by my children dependent on how much autism understanding each professional has had. A professional without sufficient (good) autism/PDA training can escalate an already distressing situation, and because of this I would advocate emergency service involvement as an absolute last resort.

Should you consider the assistance of emergency services to be necessary at some point, it can be beneficial to have a pre-prepared crisis plan that can be given to professionals on attendance. Such a plan could detail how best to communicate or interact with your child, what strategies are helpful and what strategies are likely to escalate a situation.

As a generalization, the police service has a propensity to use force to contain a situation. They can use restraint, handcuffs and deploy tasers should they consider this appropriate. As a parent, we may know that our child requires to be simply left alone to de-escalate, but an untrained police officer may make an immediate risk assessment and use force on our children.

Use of force on an autistic person in distress is unlikely to suddenly stop a neurological meltdown. While there are some children who find deep pressure comforting when in crisis, there are many others who would find touch painful when in distress – restraint in crisis is therefore likely to escalate their distress even further.

Regardless of our children's sensory preferences, what does restraint teach our children about dominance, power and control? Whoever is physically strongest wins? The most powerful can control the weak? For our children who have an anxiety-based need to remain in control, disempowering them through brute force will only breed distrust, fear and even greater anxiety.

Chapter 7

Working with Professionals

I want to begin this chapter by stating that there are some brilliant professionals who genuinely understand autism and anxiety. I will be forever grateful to my eldest son's secondary school SENCo, who respected my account of my son's presentation and supported him through the diagnostic process. While overseeing my son's education, he was a true advocate who spoke with great knowledge of my son's needs and empowered myself, as his mother, to also advocate for my son. I highly doubt that my son would have had his needs met (at all) within the education system without his input.

However, it is worth remembering that professionals are not there in a friendship capacity, even though they may behave in a friendly and supportive manner. They all have a responsibility to safeguard children.

Some families find themselves exposed to allegations of 'fabricated and induced illness' or investigated for emotional harm while trying to acquire the correct diagnosis for their autistic/PDA child, because of the current lack of professional knowledge surrounding the intersection between autism, anxiety and demand avoidance. But this is changing. More professionals are becoming aware of how best to support children with demand avoidance, thanks to the work of many great PDA advocates who have opened up the discussion around PDA nationally.

In rare circumstances, the focus for professional enquiry can be on safeguarding rather than on providing specific autism and demand avoidance support.

Acceptance of PDA as a presentation varies geographically. The National Autistic Society (UK) recognizes that pathological demand avoidance is a distinct sub-section within the autism spectrum. PDA does not yet, however, feature as a distinct diagnostic classification within the international and American diagnostic manuals, but it is increasingly common for an assessment and diagnosis to recognize a PDA presentation as part of autism. Some diagnostic pathways will clearly use the term 'pathological demand avoidance' in a diagnostic manner, whereas other pathways will refer to 'extreme demand avoidance' or 'entrenched demand avoidance' as part of an autism assessment. It is always worth asking for further clarity regarding descriptors such as these as it is my understanding as a parent that regional NHS diagnostic services each have individual positions regarding PDA as an 'official condition'. It can often be the case that families are offered contrasting opinions, or even diagnostic categorizations, from the professionals working with these children.

I recall supporting my eldest son through his autism assessment and speaking with the assigned clinical psychologist, only to be told that PDA (as a separate diagnosis) is pure invention and that there is no diagnostic difference from the condition formerly known as 'Asperger's Syndrome'. When I sought educational support later, an independent educational psychologist advised that my son be supported through the application of PDA techniques. Likewise, with my youngest son, some professionals refer to him as autistic with co-existing anxiety. Some refer to him as autistic with 'entrenched demand avoidance' but state that is *not* the same as PDA. And other professionals refer to him as autistic, with pathological demand avoidance as a subsection of his autism.

This is all incredibly confusing for both us as parents and for a child, who needs to feel secure and comfortable with their identity. It can also make working with professionals extremely complex, particularly if they do not recognize PDA as a specific and separate autistic presentation. It makes securing the right type of provision and support for our child incredibly difficult too. I have encountered professionals who have good autism knowledge but who do not recognize that for a PDA child an adapted approach is needed. When professionals do not recognize the specific support requirements necessary to allow a PDA child equal access to life (education, healthcare, leisure), it places parents, as advocates for our children, in an unnecessary conflictual position with professionals, which is counterproductive in helping PDA children to be happy.

It is likely that, as parents of an autistic child with demand avoidance, we are going to be working with professionals for long periods of time. For our children to live happy and fulfilling lives, they need access to education and friendships as much as every other child. Demand avoidance can be a huge barrier to accessing the traditional environments where these needs are met (i.e. school). For that reason, many families both seek out and are sought out by children's social care and children's mental health services in order to support access to education and enable the children to lead fulfilling lives. At times, this can feel

intrusive and frustrating for families, especially if there is a lack
of parent/professional consensus around PDA as an identified
need. This then has consequences regarding the effectiveness
of any support offered. Navigating this disparity of theoretical
understanding is key to obtaining the best outcome for your
child, and so this chapter is about how best to advocate for
your child when facing professional misunderstanding or lack
of understanding around demand avoidance.

Parental presentation

However exhausted we are, however frustrated we are by the
seemingly endless cycle of form filling and waiting lists, however desperate we are for our children's needs to be recognized,
and however emotionally raw we feel from all of this, we must
approach all interactions with professionals in a measured, civil
and professional manner. When professionals are speaking with
us directly, we need to present in a collaborative manner – we
are seeking their expertise on how best to move forwards. We
may not always agree with suggestions or observations, but being
open to hearing what is on offer is the basis of positive, ongoing
relationships. It can feel at times that professional questions are
irrelevant, but there will be a purpose. It can be very difficult
to remain emotionally neutral when discussing our children,
particularly in relation to their distress, and to a certain extent we
need to demonstrate that we have these natural, parental emotions, but it is better to discuss our emotions in a calm manner.

Ideally, it is best to approach all interactions with professionals in a business-like manner. If questions are posed that
seem irrelevant or too open-ended and without context, ask the
professional to rephrase or explain what information they are
wanting to find out with that question. As an autistic woman

myself, I can be regularly bemused by professional questioning as it takes me a week of post-conversation processing to ascertain what their intentions were in asking a specific question. I have learned that the best way to approach this difficulty is to ask them for clarity, but also to be honest in explaining that I will refer back to them when I have considered their question fully.

As parent advocates, we need to strike a balance between engaging with professional help and advocating for child-specific solutions without this being perceived as obstructive. It can sometimes be useful to support our input with sourced, objective information – advice from relevant charities, academics or organizations that advocate well for PDA children. Presenting our arguments as additional professional input in this way can often be useful in counteracting any dismissal of parental views.

As parents, we need to demonstrate that we have taken the time to educate ourselves about autism and demand avoidance, and that we have a good understanding of our children's needs – this shows that we are capable and responsible parents. However, we must be mindful not to use over-medicalized or expert language as that might appear as if we are over-complicating matters.

When parental opinion differs from professional opinion, it can be incredibly frustrating. From a parental perspective, differences of opinions regarding a child's needs do nothing but slow down progress. As parents, we have detailed knowledge of our children and can often instinctively know whether a support strategy will work or fail. As parents, we also recognize that applying the wrong type of support or intervention strategy to our child is likely to cause them unnecessary distress and potential emotional harm.

Depending on the existing parental-professional relationship, it could be beneficial to share your reasons for having doubts regarding a strategy or intervention. In doing so, it is wise to frame your concerns with reference to a supporting piece of independent evidence. Supporting evidence does not need to be from a separate, independent person but could be from some open-source, credible and academic research.

My advice would be never to disengage with a service because of differences of opinions. It is always noted and stays attached to records.

A good professional should be open to working in a restorative and problem-solving manner with parents because that is in the best interests of any child.

However, the route to acquiring any support or needs assessment for an autistic child can often be difficult due to funding and bureaucracy. In my experience (and in observing the experiences of other families), the most useful support and assessments are accessed only on completion of prior interventions, such as family therapy or parenting courses. Once these first-tier services have been utilized, and with needs for our children still observable, referrals to other avenues become easier to obtain. Finding yourself contained within this loop and being unable to access what your child really needs is, again, incredibly frustrating. A wise professional once said to me, 'Take only what you need from these first-tier services; ignore what does not suit your child or your family.' First tier-services are a gateway to other, potentially beneficial support. Trust your instincts and do not apply any suggestion that you feel will be harmful to your child. Pick and apply suggestions that are likely to be helpful, based on your expert knowledge of your child.

If it is becoming increasingly difficult to access specific pathways of support, progress for your child isn't happening, and relationships with professionals are becoming difficult, then it may be useful to undertake a request to access the information recorded about your child and your family by services you are involved with (a subject access request). Gaining this information can be useful for many reasons. It may contain information that can support a referral or application to a more appropriate service. It may provide a more transparent analysis of how professionals view your child and family. Experience has taught me to use information requests as infrequently as possible. It is definitely useful to obtain full records relating to your child from the services you are involved with – inaccurate recording of your child's needs can have lifelong implications – but if these requests are made too frequently, it could detract from the overall aim of accessing the right support for your child.

I have undertaken three major information requests for my children (child and adolescent mental health services, special education needs department and full medical records). Each request brought multiple pieces of information relating to my children that I had not been made aware of from the professionals involved at the time, one being that my son has hypermobility. This information was significant with relation to his presentation, as it enabled a fuller understanding of his fine-motor control skills, and it had further implications relating to how professionals should respond to 'challenging behaviour' (i.e. being hypermobile requires that careful consideration should be undertaken before applying certain interventions such as restraint).

The process of acquiring the correct support and help for your PDA child varies greatly from region to region. Each region will have slightly differing local policy with regards to autism and 'complex needs' provision. It can be useful to take the time and research what your local policy guidelines are; explore local government, education and healthcare provision.

(For clarity, I am writing from experience of UK-specific organizations, but the general principles will be applicable to other countries.)

Local services are guided by overall national policy and guidelines, but very often local areas issue their own local policy guidelines which they adhere to. Local branches of relevant charities may be able to help navigate how a particular area operates. Local support groups and your own GP will also have good local knowledge regarding what specific support pathways are available in your area.

Some knowledge of national SEN law is useful for when or if it becomes necessary to advocate for your child to access a service or provision. Having a basic knowledge of SEN law has previously enabled me to successfully challenge gatekeeping strategies by quoting national law in response. When I applied for my youngest child to be assessed for an EHCP, I was told that this was not possible because he did not (at that time) have a full diagnosis. I argued that the threshold for undertaking an EHC assessment was that a child may have additional needs and that I had demonstrated that sufficiently.

Guidelines from relevant expert bodies can also be used to challenge professional decision making, when necessary. There are national guidelines relating to education, children's mental health, autism assessment and provision, healthcare and social care – all of which may be helpful in supporting a parent to advocate for their child's needs.

Staying organized

As a parent of an autistic child, you will receive paperwork irrespective of what level of professional intervention there is in your family's life.

Diagnostic reports, school reports, healthcare reports, appointment letters, funding applications, care plans and information requests are some of the regular administration that feature in our home. Unfortunately, and writing from personal experience, there is very little that can be thrown away. Keeping a consistent paper trail of your child's progression (diagnosis, education and support) will provide you with strong evidence should you ever require it. And it is for this reason that I strongly recommend that all communication with professionals be via email, so there remains a trail of evidence to highlight what has taken place over the course of time.

A good filing system is imperative. Finding time to do this is difficult but can really help at a later date when your latest application for x, y or z requires yet another piece of evidence. My children have a tendency to tear paper when they are in distress, so it's wise to safeguard any filing system against potential damage. (I keep a pile of scrap paper in the kitchen for the sole purpose of paper tearing, and place the important documents in storage boxes under my bed.)

Governments and local government focus on funding and, in my experience, tend to offer generalized provision rather than the specialist and unique provision necessary to support a child with autism/PDA. In my experience, it is very difficult to acquire this type of individual support package and it may be necessary to demonstrate exactly what is necessary – by demonstrating what strategies haven't worked, what professional suggestions have been made, and what has been offered in the past. This will need to be evidenced and is why I keep written copies of all correspondence and discussion.

Try to document all discussion and conversation with services. Requesting that you are contacted via email in the first instance is a good way to do this.

By stating clearly at the beginning of the working relationship that, as parent, you do not conduct conversations on the telephone (and then following this through with not answering telephone calls), it is possible to manoeuvre discussion into a written format. In the past, I have let professionals leave a voicemail message and then I have returned their contact via email. If I have been caught by surprise (telephone contact from a mobile number, for example), then I ensure I make detailed notes, followed by an email back to the professional containing these notes, as minutes of the conversation.

A professional's minutes may focus on generalizations or their analysis of a meeting rather than factual details of what was discussed, and for this reason some parents choose to record telephone conversations or make audio recordings of meetings. I would advise any parent who is considering this course of action to research local policy guidelines and the legality of making audio recordings. A recording should be made with the consent of all those in a meeting. Because meetings are likely to be stressful and emotionally charged for parents, it is often difficult to attend to verbal contributions, advocate well, and take useful written minutes. For this reason, making recordings for your own personal use can be especially useful and so it is worth requesting consent to record as a reasonable adjustment for yourself. (Any recordings made in a professional meeting should remain for your own personal use and should never be shared in the public arena, and this includes not sharing on social media support groups.)

Meeting support

Supporting my two autistic children through formal education has meant attending many, many multiple meetings.

Sometimes these meetings have occurred every week, and on some occasions I have needed to attend two meetings in one day. It is emotionally draining and I'm not entirely sure that professionals truly understand how difficult it is to be constantly performing in the role of advocate. It is notoriously difficult to explain how demand avoidance operates on a daily basis when a significant number of professionals still believe such presentations are behavioural.

It is possible to request reasonable meeting adjustments for yourself, as any professional should agree that parental support in this context is likely to maintain positive engagement with the process.

Simple adjustments that professionals can make to help parents manage their own needs include:

- Giving timely warning of meeting dates, times and venues, and timely warnings of any changes.

- Sending an agenda for each meeting at least 48 hours in advance.

- Providing parents with minutes from the meeting in good time, following a meeting.

- Allowing audio recordings to be made to ease the pressure of parents having to make their own notes during the meeting.

- Speaking clearly and without the use of technical language.

- Taking each action point at a gentle pace.

- Allowing a short break for parents to maintain composure.

- Allowing a person to attend in support of a parent – this could be a professional advocate or scribe, or equally, a supportive friend or family member.

The better meetings I have attended have been improved by having a support professional for myself also in attendance. Unfortunately, with funding issues and diary commitments, having such support has been a luxury rather than the essential requirement that it truly is.

I find meetings extremely difficult to manage. I struggle to follow the pace at which the professionals lead and I struggle to understand what is being said by implication rather than by direct language. I struggle to multitask in terms of providing articulate responses while simultaneously making written notes. I struggle with processing all the verbal information and responding with accurate information in the timescale of the meeting. My preference is to follow up each meeting with an email response, and I ask for those further email responses to be filed alongside the meeting minutes.

My advice is to restrict email correspondence to one particular subject, and not refer to multiple issues within one email. Construct a clear subject heading and write in a business-like style. Try to compose succinct emails and include only the necessary detail.

As an autistic woman, I have a tendency to focus on details and this has led me to write very lengthy emails. Detailed focus is a good skill to have but, from a busy professional perspective, it can make emails very time-consuming to read. I have had to actively learn how best to create effective emails.

In an ideal world, asking for reasonable adjustments would not be necessary. True inclusion is considered from the outset, through good design. However, and regardless of whether a parent is neurodiverse, they are still likely to be exhausted, frustrated and emotional from having to constantly navigate support services while providing day-to-day care, and be very much in need of these reasonable adjustments for themselves.

Advocacy for a child

There may come a point at which parental input and views are no longer supported by the professional team around a child. It may be that long-standing different views regarding best approaches for progression become barriers themselves to progression.

Mediation services or advocacy services may be able to provide a way to talk through these issues and develop a positive plan to move forwards.

Another way around this situation is to instruct an independent advocate directly for your child. (Social workers and court guardians position themselves as independent but, without specialist knowledge of PDA, may not be the best advocates for your child.) Independent advocates can be hired privately but there are many charities that offer children's advocacy services – especially with regards to child protection and education, health and care plans. A children's advocate is a different type of support; they act for a child, aside from both parents and professionals. For this reason, they can provide a vital service. When choosing an advocate, ensure that they are skilled in relation to PDA, anxiety and autism as the advocate will need to elicit the views of a child in order to then present those views in meetings. The views of a child can be ascertained in numerous ways – through drawings, Talking Mats, consensual video recordings, letters – and a good advocate should be creative and flexible when obtaining these views.

The most beneficial reason for instructing a children's advocate is that they have no agenda other than representing a child's wishes and feelings. Professionals work within their own, specialized remit. For example, a school professional will be working with their budget and in-house skillset in mind. It is the same with mental health services. Funding and staff are in short supply and decision making with regards to available provision can often be based on what is available 'in house' rather than what a child actually needs. An independent advocate is not bound by these restrictions and can provide a crucial role in obtaining the correct needs-based support.

Complaints and when to use them

There may come a point at which you feel, as a parent, that progress for your child has stalled. It could be that a service has not accepted a referral, or it may be that unhelpful interventions have been applied.

When considering whether to make an official complaint, it is wise to first establish objective fact and seek an objective second opinion – advocacy agencies may be able to help here. Provide as much independent evidence in support of your position as possible. Refer to any supporting correspondence and cross-reference this with supporting diagnostic reports and care plans.

Seek as much independent advice as you can prior to lodging a complaint. Charities, ombudsmen and expert solicitors can all provide you with an objective opinion as to whether a complaint is the correct approach to take. They may also be able to assist you with following the correct complaints procedures. (Complaints can often be rejected when they have not been issued using the requested format.)

Complaints should be fully considered and made without

emotion. They should focus on fact, and reference the relevant policy guidelines and law, and state how the service or individual has failed to adhere to these standards.

A complaint can be strengthened by obtaining letters of support from charities, local councillors or your local Member of Parliament. Complaints can be strengthened further if instigated by a group of people who have shared the same experience or whose children have been treated in the same way. There is a lot of benefit in working with other families who have experienced similar treatment by the same professional or service, as the complaint is likely to be viewed as more credible.

A well-constructed, well-placed and well-timed complaint can move matters along in a positive manner.

To summarize, approach any decision to lodge a complaint with caution. A complaint that is made without supporting evidence or reason will not be helpful in sourcing the best support for your child, and may also impact on your effectiveness in being able to acquire future support for your child.

Utilizing support groups

It can be a very lonely and isolating experience when your autistic child is not yet being properly and fully supported by the appropriate services. Navigating local services and provision can be overwhelming and frightening. Families and friends that we have known for years may just not understand why life becomes so dominated by trying to source the best help and education for our child.

Wherever you live in the world, there will be other families with autistic members nearby. And if there aren't many other autistic people nearby, the internet has the capability to bring us all together.

Autism support groups and networking pages on social media are most probably our greatest resource. There are now many PDA-specific groups and pages worldwide. General autism support groups now also have an increased understanding of PDA and demand avoidance.

Support groups and networks are filled with wonderful people who have acquired immense knowledge and experience relating to autism. Every child is different, but parents of autistic children often have similar experiences, particularly in relation to working with professionals and accessing services. My advice would be that if your parental instinct is that something suggested by a professional is uncomfortable, ask within a support group. The chances are that another family has experienced a similar situation or piece of professional advice.

Local support groups are immensely useful for understanding how your local bureaucratic systems operate. They will often know how to approach a department in order to have the best chance of accessing the services offered. A local group will understand the local policies and guidelines that a parent must navigate in order to get the correct help for their child.

I am a single parent and have been so for most of my children's lives. I have had to navigate the whole diagnostic process, schooling and mental health support systems on my own. I was incredibly nervous when I first approached my local autism parenting group – my eldest son had been told he did not require an autism assessment and I was beginning to feel like a fraud for maintaining that my child was autistic. My local social media group welcomed me and I felt strengthened by knowing that my son's situation was not unique. Many other parents had had their parenting questioned, and their assertion that their child was autistic challenged by professionals. I received an abundance of practical advice, but, most importantly, I was believed and understood. This is empowering. Use the collective skill and knowledge base of those families who have already worked hard to acquire the best for their child. The exhaustion that comes from consistently having to 'fight' for your child's equal access to basic rights such as education is disabling for parents. Make this journey easier for yourself (and your child) by utilizing the collective knowledge of others.

A Final Note from the Author

The journey through having your child's needs recognized to having the right support in place is different for every family. At times, difficulties will be encountered and at others you will achieve great things on behalf of your child.

Please remember that when times are difficult, situations and circumstances change. The difficulties will not remain difficult forever.

When trying to do the very best for our children, it is also very easy to lose sight of who we are as individuals. Our own personal dreams and hopes are often suppressed in order to focus on navigating the system. We need to look after ourselves in order to continue being fantastic advocates for our children. This is a cliché, but undertaking some small activity just for our own pleasure is crucial to keeping life in perspective.

Our children are amazing. At the very beginning of my children's route to assessment, a professional suggested I keep a gratitude journal – and with each little adventure outside, or time spent playing, 1 would take a picture. Looking back through these images really does help to keep me focused on what really matters – our children's happiness.

Index